RUSSO-JAPANESE RELATIONS AND THE FUTURE OF THE U.S.-JAPANESE ALLIANCE

Harry Gelman

T0166312

Prepared for the
United States Air Force

RAND

This report addresses the implications for the American-Japanese alliance that may flow from the evolution of Moscow's relationship with Tokyo over the next decade. To this end, it traces the factors that have perpetuated the territorial dispute between Russia and Japan for many years, and their consequences for the U.S. alliance with Japan. The study examines the reasons for the cancellation of Russian President Yeltsin's September 1992 visit to Tokyo, and considers the implications of the differing policies now pursued by America and Japan toward Russia. The study weighs the possible consequences for the Japanese-American relationship if the Russian-Japanese stalemate continues. Finally, it considers the implications for the United States and Japan if Moscow and Tokyo eventually arrive at a territorial settlement. The study considers information available through December 1992.

This report was prepared as part of the National Security Strategies Program of Project AIR FORCE. The project is entitled "Russo-Japanese Relations and the Future of the U.S.-Japanese Alliance." The study should be of interest to USAF officers and others in the policy and intelligence communities concerned with the dynamic factors that could affect U.S. interests and the U.S. presence in the Western Pacific and East Asia over the next decade.

RAND is a nonprofit institution that seeks to improve public policy through research and analysis. In partnership with RAND, the Department of Defense sponsored this research to add to the available literature on this subject and prompt a wider debate than is possible based exclusively on internal DoD sources.

This RAND publication should not be construed as reflecting the opinions or policies of the Department of Defense. This report was reviewed by DoD prior to publication solely to ensure that it does not contain classified information, that it is factually accurate with respect to defense information, and it does not misrepresent official U.S. policies or plans concerning the countries involved.

CONTENTS

The cancellation of Russian President Yeltsin's September 1992 visit to Tokyo dramatized the difficulties that have long beset Russo-Japanese relations and the important consequences those difficulties have brought to America's relationship with Japan. For many years prior to the demise of the Soviet Union, the American security tie to Japan—and the U.S.-Japanese relationship as a whole—were greatly sustained by the Soviet military buildup adjacent to Japan and by the refusal to discuss the return of the "Northern Territories," four islands north of Hokkaido claimed by Japan and held by the Soviet Union since the end of World War II.

The Soviet leaders traditionally saw their occupation of the Northern Territories as legitimized, among other things, by the 1944 Yalta agreement between the USSR and three Western powers. The Soviets in the past, and the Russians today, have also maintained that these disputed islands are part of the Kuril chain, and that Japan relinquished all claim to the Kurils in the 1951 San Francisco peace treaty between Japan and most of its World War II opponents. The Japanese have traditionally countered that they did not sign the Yalta agreement and that the Soviets did not sign the San Francisco treaty. Japan has also contended that all four of the disputed islands are in any case not part of the Kuril chain.

In the 1970s and the first half of the 1980s, Soviet intransigence reinforced Japanese readiness to expand security cooperation with the United States, which became increasingly important for U.S. naval operations in the Pacific. In turn, the military alliance for a long time served as a bulwark for the Japanese-American relationship, helping to offset the threat to the relationship created by growing economic friction.

However, the momentous events of recent years—Gorbachev's geopolitical retreats, the collapse of the Soviet Union, and the crippling of Russian military power—have now undermined the common anti-Soviet rationale for the alliance. The task of articulating a new rationale and consolidating a new public consensus for this purpose may become particularly difficult in the United States, and has been complicated by the perpetuation of the Japanese quarrel with Russia over a Japanese national interest—the territorial dispute—not shared by America.

THE REASONS FOR SOVIET RECALCITRANCE

In the past, several factors traditionally served to paralyze Soviet policy and prevent the USSR from making the concessions needed to resolve the territorial issue with Japan. One was the fear of setting a precedent that other states might use to press irredentist territorial claims against the Soviet Union. Even after the end of the Soviet Union, the existence of acute disputes with other former Soviet nations around the Russian periphery continues to be one factor inhibiting Russian territorial concessions to Japan.

In addition, Soviet inflexibility was perpetuated by pessimism about the scope of the payoff for major concessions. Soviet policymakers always feared that they would not get a commensurate quid pro quo for yielding the islands, in terms of the help the Japanese would or could render to the Soviet economy. Even more important was skepticism about the rewards that major concessions to Japan would bring in terms of disruption of the Japanese-American security relationship, a traditional goal of Soviet policy. The Soviet leaders, especially in the late Brezhnev period, came to see Tokyo as an undetachable appendage to U.S. policy in the American global struggle with the Soviet Union. This gloomy intransigence of Politburo policy toward Japan was fed by an alliance of civilian conservatives and assertive military leaders who dominated the policy-formulation process and effectively suppressed dissenting opinions.

On the military side, there were several reasons for obstinacy that survive in Russia to this day. Some military leaders, like many civilian nationalists, were simply unwilling to abandon territory they saw as legitimate booty taken from Japan as a consequence of World War II. Naval commanders claimed that the southern Kurils were essential to the Soviet Union because they offered an important passage for egress to the Pacific for the Soviet Far East Fleet that the USSR had lacked during World War II. The Russian Navy has more recently also claimed that loss of the southern Kurils would constrain Russian land-based aircraft from reaching approaching U.S. carriers because "Japan's Air Defense System will be significantly expanded to the north and our aircraft do not have the combat radius to fly around it." Finally, probably the most important military consideration since the late 1970s has been concern over the use that might be made of the islands in hostile hands to facilitate antisubmarine operations against ballistic missile submarines in the Sea of Okhotsk. In this connection, the Russians now publicly acknowledge that they have important intelligence sensors in the Northern Territories which they do not want to give up.

THE FAILURE OF GORBACHEV'S RECONCILIATION EFFORTS

During the second half of the 1980s, Gorbachev made the most significant attempt since Khrushchev's time to break the impasse with Japan, but failed, largely because his efforts were too little and too late. He gave priority to his work to radically improve relations with the United States, Western Europe, and China, and to this end made significant geopolitical concessions in each case. He never felt able to make concessions of comparable importance to Japan. He did, however, make vigorous efforts to improve the atmosphere of the Japanese relationship. He purged the leading Soviet obstructionists, sent his foreign minister and other emissaries to Tokyo, multiplied contacts at many levels, acknowledged that there was in fact an unresolved territorial dispute, and agreed to begin discussions about that dispute.

After 1988, Gorbachev sought to entice the Japanese to settle for something less than half a loaf. He sent up repeated trial balloons, holding out unofficial offers to revive Khrushchev's 1956 pledge (abandoned in 1960) to return the two smallest and least important of the four islands, Shikotan and the Habomais, once a peace treaty was signed. Gorbachev hoped that a settlement on this basis would open the door to substantial Japanese loans and investments to rescue the Soviet economy.

For their part, the Japanese had become increasingly concerned that their impasse with Moscow would lead to Japan becoming isolated on the world scene, left behind by the sweep of dramatic events that was producing Sino-Soviet rapprochement and an end to the traditional American and West European hostility toward the USSR. The Japanese therefore softened their earlier demand for simultaneous return of all four islands, conceding that return of the two larger islands, Kunashiri and Eturofu, could be significantly delayed if Moscow recognized Japanese "residual sovereignty" over all four islands. But they refused to accept Gorbachev's two-island offer without this acknowledgment of sovereignty over all four.

More important, on the eve of Gorbachev's April 1991 visit to Japan, the Japanese elite for the first time was willing to spell out to Moscow details of the economic quid pro quo Moscow might expect in return for acceptance of a territorial settlement on Japanese terms. In March, secretary-general of the ruling Liberal Democratic Party (LDP) Ichiro Ozawa carried to Moscow a massive package of some $26 billion in economic benefits offered in exchange for such a settlement. By this time, however, the cumulative effect of the loss of the Soviet empire, the disruption of the Soviet economy, and the disintegration of the Soviet state had made Gorbachev far too weak politically to accept this deal. His visit to Tokyo the following month was therefore foredoomed to fail.

ILLUSORY EXPECTATIONS OF YELTSIN

In the aftermath of the collapse of the August 1991 Moscow coup, expectations were voiced in many quarters that conditions had now become much more favorable for a settlement of the territorial dispute and for a breakthrough in relations between Moscow and Tokyo. There was a general belief that there had been a big shift in the balance of Soviet political power as a result of the failure of the coup, and a reduction in the General Staff's ability to obstruct prospective territorial concessions to Japan. Many observers assumed that the replacement of the weak and vacillating Gorbachev at the heart of the policy process by the radical and apparently more forthright Yeltsin, the hero who had defeated the coup, would at last make possible decisive steps to close the gap with Japan.

However, other factors over the next year were to create imposing new barriers to a Russian-Japanese settlement. Once he took power, Yeltsin's domestic political strength, so imposing at first, was necessarily a gradually diminishing asset. The longer the economic crisis went on, and the more painful the consequences of his attempts to move toward a market economy, the more vulnerable he would become, and the harder it would therefore be to make big concessions to Japan. To make progress on his overall agenda he would have to accept grave risks on many fronts, and he could not face the consequences of trying to do so everywhere.

In addition, Yeltsin was forced to deal with the emotional consequences of the collapse of what had really been a Russian empire. The dissolution of the USSR meant the end of long-established Russian control over many nations adjacent to Russia in the borderlands of the former Soviet Union, from the Baltics to the Caucasus. Because of this humiliation there has been rapid growth of a Russian ultranationalist trend in Moscow, which came to embrace not only the old right wing but also broad sectors of the old democratic movement. One result has been a growing inflexibility about further retreat from territory anywhere around the Russian periphery—including concessions toward Japan on the Kurils issue.

Meanwhile, in the new Yeltsin era Japan declined to retreat further from the position on the territorial issue it had taken with Gorbachev, and continued to insist that large-scale economic aid could come only after the territorial question was resolved. Japanese leaders were not oblivious to the urgent Western arguments for helping Yeltsin, nor to the costs that may ultimately be paid by all if the painful effort to transform Russia is allowed to collapse for lack of sufficient Western support. But both economic and political considerations made Japan reluctant to respond.

On the economic side, most Japanese business and government leaders tended to share the view of Western skeptics that no amount of external help would stabilize the political and economic situation in Russia. At the same time, the business community was on the whole not interested enough in trade and investment opportunities in Russia to be motivated to exert strong pressure on the government to change course. Indeed, many business leaders, faced by the lack of Russian infrastructure in many areas and what they see as a discouraging environment for profitable investment, apparently were privately relieved that the Foreign Ministry's recalcitrance provided them with an excuse for not investing in Russia. Consequently, the Japanese governing elite has seen China and other areas of Asia as more promising recipients of both aid and investment funds.

These perceptions were both influenced and reinforced by the animosities generated on the political side. Many in the Japanese elite cannot see the issue of succoring democracy and moderation in Russia in the same terms as does the West, because Japan, unlike Western Europe and the United States, still has a specific national interest at stake which Russia has not satisfied. Many in Tokyo have therefore resented Western insistence that Japan give large-scale help to Russia, as tending to undermine Japanese negotiating leverage on Russia.

THE U.S. SPLITS FROM JAPAN ON AID TO YELTSIN

Against this background, pressure began to build in Washington during the early spring of 1992 for the United States to take a more active role in leading the West to help Russia avert crisis. In meetings of the seven largest industrial states (the G-7), the United States switched its position to help Europeans override Japanese objections and establish a $24 billion package of multilateral and bilateral funds for Russian balance of payments support and ruble stabilization. Compelled to participate in funding the multilateral part of this package channeled through the International Monetary Fund (IMF) and the World Bank, Tokyo reacted with anger and dismay. Although as it turned out much of the package was not in fact delivered to Moscow in 1992 because of Russian economic and political disarray, Japan initially saw this package as tending to undercut its leverage on Russia on the territorial issue. Japanese Foreign Ministry officials lamented that here had been "a U.S. policy change" that would have "a very negative effect on the negotiations between Japan and Russia."

Obliged by the West to retreat, Japanese leaders now sought to draw a firmer distinction between Japanese assistance to Russia flowing through international organizations and direct bilateral Japanese aid to Russia. Japan, they said, would now take a two-track approach, supporting decisions to provide Russia with funds from the IMF and the World Bank, but refusing to provide important new help directly from Japan unless the Northern Territories issue was resolved.

THE ROAD TO CANCELLATION OF THE YELTSIN VISIT

During the two months between the July Munich G-7 summit meeting and Yeltsin's scheduled September 1992 visit to Japan, trends in both Moscow and Tokyo made the possibility of an accommodation even more dubious. In Russia, because of the economic hardship that had accompanied the government's faltering efforts to move toward a market system, Yeltsin's political support had been sinking and the conservative opposition was rapidly growing. Ironically, the same internal pressures that made Russia badly need Japanese help also made it increasingly difficult for Yeltsin to offer sufficient concessions to Japan to get that help.

Moreover, Yeltsin's control over his military had also become uncertain. He could assert himself when he was willing to spend his political capital to do so—for example, on arms control matters. But he was far more cautious in dealing with the pugnacious line publicly adopted by many generals on nationality and territorial issues—obviously because here the military seemed to find powerful backing from the extreme nationalist tendencies growing in the civilian elite.

Yeltsin's problems with the military, when combined with his broader political difficulties, played a major role in the internal Russian struggle over Yeltsin's forthcoming trip to Japan. In the summer of 1992, the Supreme Soviet debated the Japanese question, and Russia's military leaders made a frontal appeal to Yeltsin's adversaries in parliament to cancel the troop cuts he had promised in the Kurils and to avoid any territorial concessions to Japan. The military broadside proved useful to intransigents in the legislature, who sought to force Yeltsin to cancel the Japan visit unless he was prepared to guarantee in advance to make no concessions of any kind in Tokyo. Although until the last minute Yeltsin resisted this pressure, he was driven in the end to yield because the negotiations between Russia and Japan during the weeks leading up to the scheduled visit had reached an impasse.

Probably the most striking feature of these negotiations was an event that did not happen. The Japanese governing elite remained unwilling to repeat to Yeltsin, even privately and informally, the proposal Ozawa had made to Gorbachev in 1991 spelling out the economic reward that would follow *if* the Japanese political demands regarding the Northern Territories were accepted. This behavior suggested doubt that recovery of the Northern Territories was, in fact, important enough to be worth a large Japanese economic sacrifice. It also implied some complacency about the status quo, reflecting a vague assumption that the continuation of tensions with Russia would somehow serve to postpone new problems for the U.S. alliance.

Meanwhile, Yeltsin faced a dilemma. To proceed with the visit to Japan and there formally endorse even Khrushchev's two-island concession, while leaving the fate of the other two islands open—as his Foreign Ministry wished him to do—was to accept major adverse domestic political consequences while still failing to secure an early peace treaty, a territorial settlement, or an adequate Japanese economic recompense. To go to Tokyo and leave with little to show for it but continued stalemate on the territorial issue was to invite comparison with the weak Gorbachev and Gorbachev's futile 1991 visit. But to cancel the visit outright was to give comfort to his domestic political enemies who had long sought to compel him to take that action. On the other hand, Russia had good reason to believe that because of Western pressure on Japan, those very limited economic assistance measures Japan had already arranged for the summit would be forthcoming whether the summit took place or not—as indeed subsequently proved to be the case.

In the end, after hesitating until the last minute, Yeltsin concluded that aborting the visit involved the smallest losses. As expected, Russian conservative and ultranationalist forces—both in the parliamentary opposition and within Yeltsin's own apparatus—were triumphant, while the Foreign Ministry and the progressive minority who supported it were bitter and dismayed. In Tokyo, there was considerable anger in the government and the LDP not only about the last-minute cancellation itself, but also about the rhetoric that soon emerged in Moscow blaming the cancellation on Japan. The recriminations now heard on both sides suggested that tensions between the dominant forces in the two elites had worsened, and that progress toward a settlement would be further delayed.

Although diplomatic contacts between Russia and Japan were soon resumed and both sides joined in attempting to limit the damage, a watershed was passed with the collapse of plans for the Yeltsin visit. The cancellation brought to a dismal climax the hopes of an early rapprochement that had emerged a year earlier.

Also gone were hopes that a massive infusion of Japanese capital would soon arrive in Russia to make a decisive difference in Russia's internal economic and political struggle. To be sure, there has been considerable small-scale Japanese investment activity in the Russian Far East, as well as one or two big bilateral deals permitted by Tokyo. But in general, Japanese money is not flowing to Russia on a scale relevant to the scope of Russian economic needs, nor will it until the political lock on the money is opened.

Meanwhile, Japan remains the key to Russian hopes for a revitalized relationship with East Asia, which for several decades has been the most dynamic region in the world economy. Despite much recent talk in some sectors of the Russian press about a need to shift the emphasis of foreign policy toward greater cultivation of the East, it seems unlikely that such a shift will be fruitful without a Russian modus vivendi with the dominant East Asian economy.

A final consideration is that a clock is ticking. There is reason to believe that the large Japanese pool of surplus investment capital that might potentially be made available to Russia will not remain available for long. After the middle of the decade, these surplus investment funds may diminish rapidly because of sharply rising alternative demands for investment already on the horizon, especially for huge planned Japanese domestic investment and major scheduled increases in investment and assistance in Asia. The window of opportunity for a mutually profitable territorial settlement is thus limited.

THE U.S. DILEMMA OVER JAPAN AND RUSSIA

This situation has created a growing conflict between two important American interests. One is the vested interest in the survival of a moderate, stable, and democratic government in Russia, friendly to the West, rejecting the expansionist, militarist impulses of the past, yet firmly in control of its nuclear weapons. The other is the U.S. interest in the preservation of the military alliance with Japan, until recently predicated on common hostility to Moscow, as a fundamental bulwark of the overall Japanese-American relationship. Both interests are now under threat—the first right now, the other over the next decade. The dilemma for the United States is sharpened by the fact that the evolution of events is forcing Washington to confront choices between two sets of interests it never had to make before.

This need to choose was demonstrated in the spring of 1992 when the United States saw itself compelled to split with the political interests of its Japanese ally because of its own stake in Russian stability. This was by no means the first time the United States had opposed an important Japanese interest, but it was certainly the first time since World War II that this had been done to help Moscow. When the United States shifted away from the Japanese side in the G-7 discussions over aid to Russia, it dramatized to the Japanese elite the fact that the old rationale for the Japanese-American alliance had already greatly eroded. Nothing has yet taken its place, so that the alliance is being sustained by inertia, while a widening gap has emerged between Japan's relations with Russia on the one hand, and the new relationship that the United States and other Western states have sought to build with post–cold war Russia, on the other. Although Japanese leaders wish to minimize the extent of that gap, they seem unlikely over the next year or two to retreat enough to eliminate the reality of that gap.

IF YELTSIN FALLS: RECRIMINATIONS OVER "WHO LOST RUSSIA?"

The net conclusion is that if Yeltsin and his reform program are to revive in the face of the present crisis, that will have to be accomplished without a Japanese lifeline. But there is a substantial possibility that neither Yeltsin nor his program will, in fact, long survive, and that Yeltsin may lose power entirely in the next year or two. A regime that replaced Yeltsin would be likely to be much more conservative, supernationalistic, more in the traditional Russian authoritarian mode, and reflecting much more overt influence by the military. There would probably be much more intensive efforts to restore the Russian hold on some non-Russian parts of the old Soviet Union. There would likely be a virtual end to the painful struggle toward a Western market system, and it is probable that such a new regime would be much less friendly and cooperative toward the United States and the West generally.

Throughout 1992, an increasingly plausible alternative to Yeltsin's outright replacement was that Yeltsin would manage to hold on to his title as President, but only at the cost of yielding on a much broader front than he had done before to the demands of an increasingly conservative and chauvinist opposition. During 1992 there was a significant growth of pressures on Yeltsin to retreat, to which he responded with big concessions in some areas and strong resistance in others. The cancellation of Yeltsin's visit to Japan was one of the retreats in question. By December, he had finally yielded to reactionary pressure at the Congress of People's Deputies and had abandoned Premier Yegor Gaidar. It remained to be seen how far this most drastic retreat would carry him, and to what extent the tendency toward internal reform and external moderation could survive.

If, in the end, Yeltsin either falls or becomes a total prisoner of the right, there will probably be many recriminations to follow, both inside the United States and other Western countries and between the United States and its allies. Despite the fact that the United States has itself been unwilling to make substantial sacrifices to assist Russia, Japan—because of its greater potential to help—is widely, and with some justice, regarded as the leading recalcitrant. The Japanese therefore have reason to believe that a political disaster in Moscow would trigger a widespread tendency in the West to blame Japan.

IF YELTSIN "MUDDLES ALONG": THE PRESSURES FOR U.S. INVOLVEMENT

On the other hand, there is some chance that despite the fall of Premier Gaidar, the Yeltsin regime will go on "muddling through" over the next few years with many trends in the country substantially unchanged. Under this scenario, the Russian government will continue to lean to some degree toward cooperation with the United States but will also continue to be constrained from making the concessions to Japan needed for a territorial settlement. Yeltsin, according to this hypothesis, will continue to walk a tightrope on economic policy, maneuvering between the urgings of the West on one side to press ahead with marketization and the pressure from his industrial lobby on the other side to slow it down. He will make barely enough concessions to IMF demands to keep a flow of capital coming through international channels sufficient to underwrite a minimum of imports and investments from the West. But economic progress and prospects in Russia will remain very poor, and this will be attributed by many in Russia to a lack of sufficient Western—and especially Japanese—help.

Under these circumstances, we are more likely to hear some in Moscow more vigorously press the argument that the main obstacle to return of the southern Kurils is the Russian sense of threat from the U.S. force structure in the area, coupled with the existence of the U.S. military alliance with Japan. In recent years, prior to 1992, such talk had dwindled as many Russians—and indeed, some military leaders—came to value the U.S.-Japan security treaty as reducing the possibility of a return of Japanese militarism. But in the summer of 1992, the Russian General Staff, in opposing return of the southern Kurils, justified its stance by emphasizing its alleged concerns about a potential U.S.-Japanese threat. Others on the opposite side of the Russian internal debate have also brought America into the picture on the territorial dispute, suggesting that the alliance force posture is anachronistic and plays into the hands of the Russian military leaders who have helped to block a deal with Japan. The moderate former Russian Vice Premier Mikhail Poltoranin, during his early August 1992 visit to Japan, said that he favored direct U.S. "participation in the discussion of military problems linked with the South Kurils issue."

In the United States, domestic trends could generate a significant response over the next few years to vigorous Russian appeals for a major force reduction in the area, or even for some loosening of the security relationship with Japan. Given the disappearance of the Soviet worldwide challenge and the growth of America's long-term economic difficulties and budget dilemmas, some influential American voices have already begun to suggest that much greater U.S. force reductions were needed in the western Pacific—and not only to save money, but also to facilitate a Russo-Japanese territorial settlement. It is likely that if Yeltsin survives, more such voices will be heard, in Congress as well as in the press.

SHOULD THE UNITED STATES INTERVENE?

In addition, some in the United States have already suggested that Washington should seek to mediate the territorial issue. Because of the important U.S. interest in maintaining stability in Russia, the United States has already quietly sought to encourage both sides toward mutual compromise, but with little result. There are indeed good reasons why more vigorous and sustained intervention into this matter by the new U.S. administration could prove to be in the interests of all three countries.

It is essential, however, that intervention be conducted with due regard for the American stake in preserving the alliance with Japan. Although much greater concessions by both Japan and Russia will be required, the United States cannot afford to adopt a posture of neutrality on all the issues at stake. Thus the United States would incur significant political risks if, in the interests of mediation, it were to repudiate the posture of support for the Japanese territorial claims that America has maintained up to now. Such a radical shift would come as a shock, and seem a grievous betrayal to many Japanese.

But this does not mean that the United States should remain passive toward its Russian-Japanese dilemma. The assumption that Japan and the United States can indefinitely preserve the political foundations of their alliance while ignoring their diverging interests in relations with Russia seems shortsighted. The alliance can be broadly supported in both countries only if the justification for its existence is shared. If only because of the probable demands of the U.S. public and Congress, the continued viability of Japan's military relationship with the United States must depend in the long run on finding a new basis for the alliance tied, among other things, to a common modus vivendi with Russia.

It would therefore be in the common interest if the United States, with due discretion, begins to work to encourage Japan to renew, and if possible, improve the 1991 Ozawa proposal. In this connection, a tight coordination of Washington's Russia policy and its Japan policy will be critical. America should simultaneously do what it can to encourage the emergence of a coalition in Moscow willing to bear the massive political burden of territorial concessions if shown a prospect of a sufficiently massive economic reward. But that process cannot even begin until Japan becomes willing to speak of a quid pro quo in more than evasive generalities.

In addition—but only in conjunction with the emergence of that economic quid pro quo—the United States should formally reexamine with Japan the question of the confidence-building measures (CBMs) in northeast Asia long advocated by Moscow, but traditionally opposed by the United States and Japan as tending to constrain the operations of the alliance. To some extent, this consultation process has already quietly begun, but it would be useful for it to be accelerated, so that the two allies can jointly determine which specific confidence-building measures are acceptable under the radically new strategic circumstances, and which are not. It is in the common interest of Japan and the United States to seek to reduce both the incentives and the ability of the Russian military establishment to obstruct Russian concessions in the region. To this end, it would be helpful for those CBMs found to be consistent with preservation of a viable alliance to be offered to Russia at an early date provided that this is done against the background of a major Japanese economic offer tacitly linked to a territorial settlement.

To be sure, there are potential problems attached to such a U.S. effort even aside from the great political obstacles in the Japanese and Russian elites. By the close of 1992, the Russian economic and political crisis—above all, the threat of hyperinflation, the fears of massive unemployment, and the diffusion of authority in Moscow—had grown to such an extent that some would question whether any outside economic assistance could make a major contribution to solving the crisis. In addition, there is a question about the relevant scale of assistance. Some in the West are uncertain whether the $26 billion once offered by Ozawa would now in any case be sufficient to make a meaningful dent in Russia's enormous capital needs, and for that reason have urged Japan to consider larger sums.

There is no doubt that this issue of the usefulness of Western and Japanese assistance will turn mostly on the future behavior of the Russians themselves—and to what extent the reform process can survive the events at the December 1992 session of the Congress of People's Deputies. In particular, averting the threat of hyperinflation will be one of several prerequisites for effective Russian use of any future external assistance, including any hypothetical Japanese aid package that might be associated with a territorial settlement. But given an essential minimum of Russian cooperation, appropriately directed Japanese and Western help could still make an important difference in easing the Russian transition to a market economy. Moreover, the political effects of such inputs from the industrial democracies could be at least as important as the economic effects, by reinforcing the gravely weakened political position of those in the Russian elite who have fought, against increasing odds, for both marketization and friendly ties with the West. In particular, Western and Japanese assistance is likely to help the Russian political situation to the degree that it is focused on mitigating the social effects of the unemployment that would flow from downsizing of large, money-losing military industrial enterprises.

IF A SETTLEMENT OCCURS: IMPLICATIONS FOR THE ALLIANCE

The most important long-term contingency facing the alliance is the possibility that despite the vast difficulties now in view, a Russo-Japanese territorial settlement will eventually emerge later in this decade. This event would accelerate the pressures that are already growing to reshape the mission and orientation of the alliance, to make it more open-ended and inevitably less concrete and specific, because it would be less immediately focused on Russia. The Japanese-American alliance would have to confront directly the kind of fundamental questions about its purpose which the NATO alliance has been forced to consider ever since the collapse of the USSR. These questions will be more difficult to resolve if the prolonged Japanese quarrel with Russia imposes an artificial delay in addressing the issue.

Japan for its part has several strong incentives to want to maintain the alliance. First, it remains the bulwark of the total Japanese-American relationship, helping to offset the economic tensions that exist between Japan and its most important customer. Not only the Japanese government but the Japanese business community seem convinced of this.

Second, the alliance with the United States serves as what might be termed the protective cover for Japan's economic and political relationship with its Asian neighbors. Japan's tie to the United States is generally seen as an insurance policy for Asia, helping to calm the suspicions and concerns about Japan's strength that exist almost everywhere in East Asia and that would emerge openly if not for the reassuring perception that a rebirth of Japanese militarism is held in check by Japan's military alliance with America. The Japanese leadership is well aware of this.

And third, the alliance is a guarantee for Japan itself against the unknown: that is, the possibilities of either resurrection of a Russian threat some day or emergence of some new threat (e.g., from a more assertive China, or from a new Sino-Russian alliance, or from a nuclear-armed North Korea).

The future attitude of the American public and Congress in the face of drastic geopolitical changes and grim budget realities is more problematical. A strong case can be made, however, for continuation of expenditures sufficient to preserve the alliance and maintain some American forward deployments in the region.

First, the United States itself benefits politically from the fact that most of the East Asian states are quite anxious to see the U.S.-Japanese alliance continue as a guarantee of Japanese political and military restraint. For that very reason, the existence of the alliance fortifies the welcome given by many of those states to the U.S. military presence in the region and increases their self-interest in cooperating with the United States—with support facilities, for example. In addition, many East Asians, like the Japanese, are concerned at the prospect of accelerating Chinese weapons programs and increasing Chinese assertiveness and welcome the continuation of the U.S. presence as a geopolitical counterweight. For both reasons, the continuation of an American presence tied to the Japanese alliance enhances U.S. influence in the region.

Second, despite the existence of some alternative support facilities elsewhere, the loss of the Philippine bases and the prospect of a reduced presence in Korea have made the Japanese military connection more important than ever for the U.S. geopolitical position in East Asia. The demise of the Japanese alliance would probably mean a general pullback of the United States from the Western Pacific.

Third, the United States, like East Asia, should be concerned about regional insurance against the unknown future. Americans, no less than the Japanese, have an interest in preserving the alliance as protection against unpleasant contingencies that may or may not yet be visible on the horizon. As in Europe, the Asian alliance of the United States is an investment in defense of American interests that will be affected by unknowable future developments in any case, whether or not the United States remains on the scene.

Finally, the United States, no less than the Asian states, has a national interest in preserving the alliance as a means of ensuring that the Japanese political consensus underlying Japan's restrained and cooperative military posture will endure. If some day dangerous changes do occur in the Far East, the American relationship with Japan, by reassuring the Japanese public, will reinforce the likelihood of moderation in the Japanese national reaction. One obvious such contingency would be North Korean achievement of a nuclear capability, which in the absence of the U.S. umbrella might strengthen the hand of the presently small Japanese minority that wishes to do the same.

In sum, delay and lassitude in confronting the difficulties looming ahead for the alliance are likely to be harmful. The world has changed; Japanese and American interests regarding Russia are no longer working in harmony, and are indeed now operating at cross-purposes. The United States does have an important national interest in the preservation of the alliance with Japan, and for that very reason, it now has a growing stake in working for a settlement between Japan and Russia.

ACKNOWLEDGMENTS

The author wishes to thank Paul Langer and Mike Mochizuki for their helpful comments on an early draft of this report. He also wishes to thank Vladimir Shkolnikov and Charles Wolf, Jr. for their insights on Russian-Japanese economic issues relevant to the study. The author alone should be held responsible for any errors or omissions found in the analysis.

RAND#161-01-0193

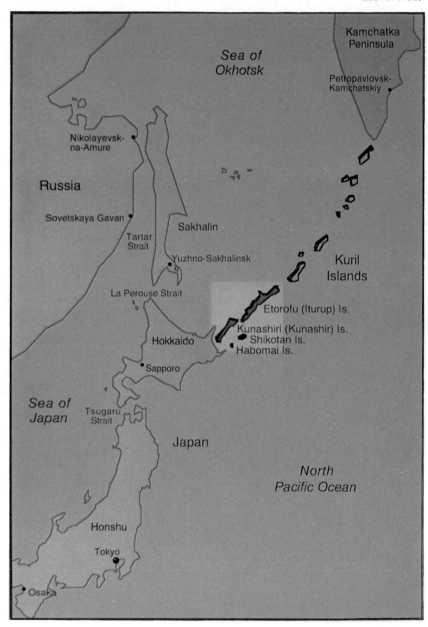

Japan, Russia, and the Disputed Territories

Chapter One

INTRODUCTION

The cancellation of Russian President Yeltsin's September 1992 visit to Tokyo again dramatized the difficulties that have long beset Russo-Japanese relations and the important consequences they have brought over the years to America's relationship with Japan. This report addresses the implications for the American-Japanese alliance that may flow from the evolution of Moscow's relationship with Tokyo over the next decade. To this end, it examines the factors that could perpetuate the impasse, as well as the chances that a radical change will eventually occur in relations between Moscow and Tokyo through arrival at a modus vivendi on the Russian-Japanese territorial issue that would open the way for a massive infusion of Japanese economic assistance to Russia. The study then examines the possible consequences for the Japanese-American relationship if this fundamental change should occur, and alternatively the consequences if it does not happen and the present Russian-Japanese impasse continues.

The report first sketches the background of the Soviet-Japanese territorial dispute and the evolution of Soviet behavior toward Japan in the pre-Gorbachev era, describing the impact of that behavior upon the Japanese-American security relationship. The study then reviews those changes introduced into Japan-Soviet relations by Gorbachev and examines the reasons why—despite the growth of Soviet need for Japanese help and the first signs of some softening in the Japanese consensus—Gorbachev was unable to resolve the territorial issue and achieve a fundamental breakthrough. The study next turns to Boris Yeltsin, traces the evolution of his attitude toward Japan before the August 1991 attempted Moscow coup, and evaluates the

1

many considerations that inhibited his policy toward Tokyo in the first year after the failure of the coup. The report concludes with a discussion of the prospects for change, and the implications for Japan and America.

Chapter Two

THE HISTORICAL BACKGROUND

THE NATURE OF THE IMPASSE

For many years prior to the demise of the Soviet Union, the American security tie to Japan—and the U.S.-Japanese relationship as a whole—were greatly sustained by the Soviet military buildup adjacent to Japan and by the refusal of Gorbachev's predecessors to discuss the return of the "Northern Territories," four islands north of Hokkaido claimed by Japan and held by the Soviet Union since the end of World War II.

The Soviet leaders traditionally saw their occupation of the Northern Territories as legitimized, among other things, by the 1944 Yalta agreement between the USSR and three Western powers. The Soviets in the past, and the Russians today, have also maintained that these disputed islands are part of the Kuril chain, and that Japan relinquished all claim to the Kurils in the 1951 San Francisco peace treaty between Japan and most of its World War II opponents. The Japanese have traditionally countered that they did not sign the Yalta agreement and that the Soviets did not sign the San Francisco treaty. Japan has also contended that all four of the disputed islands are in any case not part of the Kuril chain.

In the 1970s and the first half of the 1980s, the intransigence of Soviet policy toward Japan served to reinforce Japanese readiness to expand security cooperation with the United States, which became increasingly important for U.S. naval operations in the Pacific. In turn, the military alliance for a long time served as a bulwark for the overall Japanese-American relationship, helping to offset the threat to that relationship created by growing economic friction. Over the years since the 1970s, a long succession of Western observers freshly discovered and newly marveled at what seemed the obviously counterproductive obstinacy of Soviet policy regarding the Northern Territories, and repeatedly predicted that it was therefore about to change.

However, this did not happen throughout the lifetime of the Soviet Union because a combination of factors served to paralyze Soviet policy and to prevent the Soviet leaders from moving to satisfy the Japanese.

THE REASONS FOR SOVIET INTRANSIGENCE

One of several reasons for this Soviet paralysis was the traditional fear of setting a precedent that other states around the Soviet periphery might use to press irredentist territorial claims against the Soviet Union. The leading case in point was always the Chinese claims along the Sino-Soviet border, but the Soviets also had in mind the vulnerabilities stemming from their seizure of various territories in Europe at the close of World War II—for example, Moldavia, taken from Romania; Karelia, taken from Finland; and East Prussia, taken from Germany. It will be seen later in this study that this worry about the precedent remained in Gorbachev's time,[1] and even after the collapse of the Soviet Union this consideration has not ceased to hamper Boris Yeltsin's flexibility in dealing with Japan. The existence of acute territorial and nationality disputes with several other former Soviet nations around the Russian periphery continues to be a factor inhibiting Russian territorial concessions to Japan.

In addition, at least until well into the Gorbachev era, inertia and inflexibility were perpetuated in Moscow by a sense that there was little chance of achieving Soviet policy goals by accommodating Tokyo. Among other things, Soviet policymakers were inhibited from major concessions by pessimism about the scope of the economic payoff.

---

[1] In February 1990, Gorbachev's Foreign Ministry spokesman Gennady Gerasimov publicly acknowledged that those in the leadership who were opposed to returning the islands believed it would create a "dangerous precedent" for other postwar borders. (Gerasimov address to One Asia Assembly in Moscow, reported by Associated Press, February 20, 1990.)

They always feared that they would not get a commensurate quid pro quo from the Japanese for yielding the islands, in terms of the help the Japanese would or could render to the Soviet economy. This attitude was perpetuated by a tendency, in the pre-Gorbachev era, to underestimate the gravity of the Soviet economic crisis and therefore the extent of Soviet need for Japanese help.

Perhaps even more important was an underlying skepticism about the political and strategic rewards that major concessions to Japan would bring in terms of disrupting the Japanese-American security relationship that had emerged since World War II, a traditional goal of Soviet policy. Soviet expectations in this regard were powerfully affected by two watershed defeats for Soviet postwar policy toward Japan. The first was the failure of the Soviet campaign in the late 1950s to prevent the signing of revisions to the U.S.-Japan security treaty, the event that created the legal and political underpinning for the subsequent further growth of Japanese security cooperation with the United States against the Soviet Union. The second was the failure of the Soviet effort two decades later to prevent the signing of the Japan-China peace treaty, an agreement which Moscow at the time erroneously thought would lay the basis for a strategic alliance among the United States, Japan, and China against the USSR.

Because of these defeats and other disappointments, by the end of the 1970s the Kremlin had come to regard Japan with a peculiar mixture of disdain (because of its international political passivity), apprehension (because of its growing economic stature), and hopelessness (because of the great breadth of its links to the United States). In essence, the Soviet leadership in the late Brezhnev period saw Tokyo not as an independent actor, but as an undetachable appendage to U.S. policy in the American global struggle with the Soviet Union.

Until Gorbachev came on the scene, the gloomy intransigence of Politburo policy toward Japan was fed by an alliance of civilian conservatives and assertive military leaders who dominated the policy-formulation process and effectively suppressed dissenting policy opinions.[2] On the civilian side, until the mid-1980s there were three

---

[2] For an overview of the thinking of this apparatchik alliance, see Harry Gelman, *The Brezhnev Politburo and the Decline of Détente*, Cornell University Press, Ithaca, 1984.

leading figures who persistently stood in the way of change in policy toward Japan.

One was Politburo member Andrey Gromyko, who was generally disdainful of Japan and visited the country only once in 28 years as Foreign Minister.[3] The second was the party Central Committee apparatchik and ideologue Ivan Kovalenko, whose influence on this matter was almost as important as Gromyko's, and the third was Kovalenko's junior ally Deputy Foreign Minister Mikhail Kapitsa, who supervised Far East policy in the Foreign Ministry.

Kovalenko, who in earlier years had administered the interrogation and propaganda use of Japanese prisoners of war, had a personal contempt and hatred for Japan and was the most ardent senior advocate of maintaining pressure on Tokyo. As the deputy head of the Central Committee International Department, who was charged with providing advisory memoranda to the Politburo on Far East matters, Kovalenko for 20 years exercised extraordinary influence over the policy process, and became notorious in Japan as a symbol of Soviet inflexibility.[4]

On the military side of the military-ideologue alliance, a similar perspective was maintained by many senior commanders for a variety of reasons. On the simplest level, some military leaders, like many civilian nationalists, were simply unwilling to abandon territory they regarded as legitimate booty taken from Japan as a consequence of World War II. Some, like Chief of the General Staff Marshal Nikolay Ogarkov, justified intransigence by continuing to allude to a de facto

---

For a historical review of the evolution of their decisionmaking system, see Harry Gelman, *The Rise and Fall of National Security Decisionmaking in the Former USSR*, RAND, R-4200-A, 1992.

[3]Although there is some evidence, discussed below, that Gromyko sought briefly to revive negotiations with Japan in the détente period of the early 1970s, this was apparently an aberration, and his personal posture toward Tokyo became increasingly rigid after the mid 1970s. This attitude was evidenced, among many other things, by his support for and promotion of Deputy Foreign Minister Mikhail Kapitsa.

[4]Kovalenko was head of the Japan section of the Central Committee International Department from 1963, and a deputy chief of the Department from 1983. When Gorbachev retired him, a Japanese review of his career emphasized that Kovalenko's earlier experience in tyrannizing and attempting to brainwash Japanese war prisoners had cemented a conviction that "the Japanese listen when intimidated." *(Sankei Shimbun* (Tokyo), November 8, 1988.)

Sino-Japanese-American military alliance against the Soviet Union well after the possibility of such an alliance had disappeared. In addition, naval commanders long claimed that the southern Kurils were essential to the Soviet Union because they offered an important passage for egress to the Pacific for the Soviet Far East Fleet that the USSR had lacked during World War II.[5] This particular argument of the Soviet era was to be revived and greatly elaborated in a campaign by the Russian military leadership against the surrender of the Northern Territories in the summer of 1992. At that time, the Russian Navy also asserted that loss of the southern Kurils would constrain Russian land-based aircraft from reaching approaching U.S. carriers because "Japan's Air Defense System will be significantly expanded to the north and our aircraft do not have the combat radius to fly around it."[6]

Soviet military leaders until recently were rather reticent about acknowledging a strategic nuclear motive for wanting to retain the Northern Territories. There is little doubt, however, that for the last 15 years they have been preoccupied over the security of the ballistic missile submarine (SSBN) bastion area in the Sea of Okhotsk, bordered by the Northern Territories. After the late 1970s—when the USSR achieved the ability to reach the United States with sea-launched ballistic missiles fired from Soviet home waters—the most significant military reason for Soviet obstinacy over the Northern Territories became concern over the use that might be made of the islands in hostile hands, to facilitate antisubmarine warfare (ASW) operations against Soviet SSBNs in the Sea of Okhotsk. Although it is not clear whether the Russian military leadership in fact continues to assign the same weight to this consideration, since the summer of 1992 it has discussed the issue more openly than before.[7]

---

[5] In 1991, the reactionary nationalist politician S. N. Baburin asserted that the southern Kuril straits "are our only ice-free straits, whereas all straits between the North Kurils freeze over." Moreover, he claimed that "Kasatka Bay [in the Kurils] with its deep waters is unique from the military point of view; the Japanese Navy massed in this bay in 1941 before the attack on Pearl Harbor and the Americans were unable to detect it at the time." *(Sovetskaya Rossiya,* October 17, 1991.)

[6] *Nezavisimaya Gazeta,* July 30, 1992 (JPRS-UMA, August 12, 1992, 38-39).

[7] In July 1992, the Russian General Staff made the unprecedented public statement that "the Pacific Fleet deploys an ASW barrier along the Kuril chain in time of threat to secure the combat survivability of strategic naval forces." This barrier would be

It was during the first half of the 1980s, just before Gorbachev came to power, that the domination of Soviet policy by the alliance of military leaders with civilian ideologues reached its climax. In this period, Japan's inferiority to the Soviet Union in military power aroused the same Soviet bullying instincts that were simultaneously being displayed in Europe through the anti-INF campaign orchestrated by Gromyko's Foreign Ministry and by Kovalenko's colleagues in the Central Committee International Department. In Japan's case, the pressure was reflected, among other things, in nuclear threats and frequent air and naval territorial violations, all of which only served to reinforce Japanese resentment and to solidify the popular consensus behind the military alliance with the United States.

The assertive Soviet military posture toward Japan in the pre-Gorbachev era proved counterproductive because the Soviets could obtain little political leverage on the Japanese body politic through its Far East military buildup and the pressure implied in frequent territorial violations. In Western Europe, where the fears of nuclear war engendered by the shrill Soviet anti-INF campaign were greatly exacerbated by the visible threat posed by massive and numerically superior contiguous Soviet tank armies, a substantial domestic movement emerged pressing for Western concessions. But in dealing with Japan, the Soviets were unable to resurrect the turmoil that had existed in the late 1950s during the Japanese domestic battle over the U.S. security treaty. This failure was partly a result of the great changes that had taken place during the ensuing thirty years in the Japanese economy and society, in Japanese self-confidence, and in the Japanese relationship with America and the world. But it was partly also because of the adverse facts of geography. Unlike the situation in Europe, the Soviets had no contiguous land frontier, no means of implying a credible threat to overrun Japan, and therefore little capability to revive significant domestic pressure on the Japanese government by heightening popular anxieties.

In short, Soviet policies toward Japan in the years leading up to Gorbachev's appearance on the scene had the worst of both worlds, evoking anger but little fear. Consequently, in the same period when NATO's ability to carry out major security decisions was coming un-

---

breached, the General Staff claimed, with the surrender of any of the Kurils to Japan. (*Nezavisimaya Gazeta*, July 30, 1992 [FBIS-SOV, July 31, 1992, 26–28].)

der severe domestic challenge, Japanese public acceptance of the Self-Defense Forces and support for the American alliance continued to grow despite the simultaneous emergence of bilateral economic friction.

THE ADVENT OF GORBACHEV

In the last half of the 1980s, this comfortable situation for the United States began to erode as Gorbachev incrementally transformed Soviet global policies through monumental concessions and retreats that radically changed the traditionally threatening Soviet public image in Europe and the West generally.

That fundamental change in the Soviet posture was slower to emerge in the Far East than in Europe, and slowest of all in Soviet policy toward Japan. This lag stemmed from Gorbachev's global and regional priorities. Massive Soviet military concessions emerged first in Europe rather than in East Asia because the elimination of military confrontation with the United States and NATO was necessarily most important to Gorbachev. Meanwhile, to the degree that he did focus on policy in the Far East, Gorbachev obviously saw his first and most vital task as the effort to achieve a rapprochement with China, a long-drawn-out process that culminated with the summit meeting of 1989.[8] The most important anomaly in Gorbachev's behavior in East Asia was consequentiy the contrast between his willingness to make important and concrete concessions to the national interests of China, on the one hand, and his inability to make comparably important concessions to conciliate Japan, on the other.

Because the rapprochement with China was the centerpiece of Gorbachev's Far East endeavors, it was evidently considered to be worth some real sacrifices.[9] The Soviet leadership, in securing the June 1989 summit meeting with China, achieved a geopolitical

---

[8]See Harry Gelman, "Gorbachev and Sino-Soviet Normalization," in *Moscow and the Global Left in the Gorbachev Era*, Joan B. Urban (ed.), Cornell University Press, Ithaca, New York, 1992, 90–126.

[9]Not everyone in the Gorbachev regime agreed, however, and an early struggle went on in the Central Committee apparatus over policy toward China that was somewhat analogous to the struggle over policy toward Japan. See the revelations of one apparatchik in *Far Eastern Economic Review*, June 11, 1992.

breakthrough to which Gorbachev obviously and rightly attached a great deal of value. One of the important considerations that led the Chinese to consent to the summit and to cross this watershed in their relationship with the Soviets was the hope of securing an eventual major reduction in the forces deployed against China since 1965. Since 1987, Gorbachev had been furnishing installment payments on this tacit promise, with the incremental withdrawal of threatening Soviet forces from Mongolia, the removal of the SS-20 missiles from Asia, and the announcement of a 12-division reduction in ground forces deployed in the Far East. These steps were accompanied by adoption of a more conciliatory posture on another matter of special importance to Chinese national interests, the question of defining the Sino-Soviet border.

The contrast with the degree to which Gorbachev was willing to conciliate Japan was quite vivid. Here Soviet policy remained locked in a position similar to the one adopted toward China in the pre-Gorbachev era—a posture of offering mostly changes in style in place of large geopolitical retreats. From first to last, Gorbachev's central aim was to find a way to get the Japanese to agree to improve the atmosphere of the relationship and to greatly expand trade and investment in the Soviet Union even if he could not offer Japan an acceptable settlement of the Northern Territories question. The preferred Gorbachev strategy was therefore to radically energize political and diplomatic engagement with Japan and—in contrast with the past—to show a cooperative disposition on all inessentials while permitting only very limited movement on the issue of key importance to Japan.

This is not to say that the changes Gorbachev introduced into Soviet behavior toward Japan were insignificant. In January 1986, he broke with the past sufficiently to send Foreign Minister Eduard Shevardnadze to Tokyo, in the first visit by a Soviet Foreign Minister to Japan in over a decade. In contrast to Shevardnadze's predecessor Gromyko, the new Foreign Minister displayed an unusually pleasant demeanor to the Japanese, although for the time being he remained as inflexible as Gromyko regarding the Northern Territories. At this point, he continued to insist, like previous Soviet spokesmen, that the Northern Territories question was a nonsubject, and that there was no territorial issue between the Soviet Union and Japan.

That official public stance was maintained through much of 1988.[10] But by the time Shevardnadze returned for a second trip to Japan in December 1988, three years after his first visit, the Gorbachev regime had quietly begun to edge away from this traditional frozen posture. During a Moscow conversation between Gorbachev and former Japanese Premier Yasuhiro Nakasone in the summer of 1988, Gorbachev hinted that the Soviet Union was now willing to cease denying that a territorial issue did exist, and Shevardnadze in Tokyo again implied, although he did not yet explicitly confirm, this tactical concession. One practical consequence was that a joint Soviet-Japanese working group at vice foreign minister level was set up in the wake of the December 1988 Shevardnadze visit, empowered to consider all issues relevant to a Soviet-Japanese peace treaty—including the territorial issue.[11]

THE TWO-ISLAND ALTERNATIVE

By this time, the Gorbachev leadership in behind-the-scenes policy discussions had apparently resolved to test the possibility that Japan might be willing to settle for a weak compromise—a one-quarter loaf—on the territorial question. The compromise under consideration was the so-called "two-island alternative."

Over the years, this alternative has been a recurrent focal point for diplomatic sparring between Moscow and Tokyo. The issue at stake is whether a settlement can be reached through some formula reviving or modifying the limited territorial concession offered by Khrushchev to Japan in 1956 and subsequently withdrawn. Khrushchev had made his offer at a time when the Soviet Union was attempting to normalize its relations with Japan, and to do so in a fashion that would prevent the consolidation and extension of exist-

---

[10]As late as May 1988, Shevardnadze parroted this line to a visiting leader of the Japanese parliament: "As to the so-called territorial issue, the Soviet side regards it as solved on a historical and international legal basis. The Soviet Union has a lot of territory but not any that we do not need." (TASS, May 7, 1988.)

[11]In the joint communiqué issued with the Japanese on the visit, Shevardnadze agreed only to reiterate an October 1973 formula that said the two sides had discussed "historical and political aspects" of their disagreements. (*Pravda*, December 22, 1988.) But in at least one interview in Tokyo, he made it clear that the territorial issue would be considered by the new working group. (*Sankei Shimbun*, December 21, 1988.)

ing U.S.-Japanese security cooperation. After lengthy negotiations, Khrushchev therefore signed a Joint Declaration with Japan agreeing to return Shikotan and the Habomais—the two smallest and least important of the four disputed islands, and the two closest to Hokkaido—as a good-will gesture that would take effect upon the signing of a Soviet-Japanese peace treaty.[12] Subsequently, however, negotiations for such a treaty became indefinitely stalled because Japan would not accept the two-island formula as sufficient for a permanent territorial settlement.[13] For their part, the Soviets left this offer on the table for only a little more than three years. In January 1960, Khrushchev unilaterally (and, the Japanese say, illegally) revoked the 1956 Joint Declaration's two-island commitment in retaliation against the conclusion of the revised Treaty of Mutual Cooperation and Security between Japan and the United States.[14]

---

[12]*New York Times*, October 20, 1956. The Joint Declaration provided for recognition of the end of the war between Japan and the USSR and the renewal of diplomatic relations. Concluded after a year of sparring over Japanese demands that Kunashiri and Etorofu also be ceded as the price of a peace treaty, the declaration bypassed any mutual commitment on the territorial question, providing for the continuation of negotiations on a peace treaty without commenting on the subject of those negotiations. This formula left the Soviets subsequently free to contend that their unilateral offer in the declaration to return the Habomais and Shikotan was intended to close the territorial issue, and the Japanese free to point out that they had said nothing in the declaration to imply that.

[13]During the conversations in the summer of 1956 that led up to the Joint Declaration, the Japanese Premier had momentarily become willing to settle for a peace treaty based on a two-island solution and Japanese acceptance of Soviet sovereignty over the two largest of the four islands. Eventually, however, he was compelled to retreat from this position by a combination of intense resistance from Japanese conservatives and American objections. He therefore settled for the so-called "Adenauer formula" pioneered by the Federal Republic of Germany, in which the state of war with the USSR was ended and diplomatic relations restored without prejudice to the status of territorial borders.

[14]*Pravda*, January 29, 1960. Khrushchev took this step in a period when, under pressure from the Chinese and his own leadership ideologues, he had abandoned his initial 1959 détente with the United States and was pressing a worldwide, militant struggle against Washington. His note to Japan revoking the Habomais-Shikotan offer characteristically included the threat of nuclear "catastrophe" he was making against other U.S. allies at this time. He now insisted that Japan must accept "neutrality" and remove all foreign troops from the country before the two-island offer could be renewed. The Japanese reply to the note asserted that Khrushchev had violated international legal norms by unilaterally imposing an additional condition on an earlier bilateral commitment. (*New York Times*, January 29, 1960.)

There is fragmentary evidence to suggest that in 1972 and 1973, at the height of the short-lived Brezhnev détente with the United States, the Brezhnev regime briefly toyed with the notion of reviving the two-island proposal. Any such change was apparently blocked by military opposition.[15] Subsequently, throughout the remainder of the Brezhnev era, Soviet policy was focused on obtaining a peace treaty decoupled from the territorial question. After 1975, the Soviets sought, as a substitute, to get the Japanese to agree to a similarly decoupled "good neighbor" treaty. The Japanese strenuously resisted both notions.

It was not until after the Brezhnev era had come to an end that the Soviet leadership again became interested in pursuing the alternative Khrushchev had raised. In 1983, shortly after Yuriy Andropov came to power, two senior Japanese figures with close contacts in the Japanese government and business community were approached by Soviet contacts seeking an estimate of Japan's likely reaction to a hypothetical Soviet statement that the status of Shikotan and the Habomais might be considered unsettled. On both occasions, the Soviets were told that the Japanese reaction would be negative, that it was too late for such a partial concession, and that Japanese public opinion would no longer tolerate a deal that failed to return all four islands to Japan.[16]

---

[15]In the summer of 1992, a report attributed to "well-informed Russian diplomatic sources in Tokyo" alleged that Gromyko had raised the two-island possibility in private talks with Japanese Foreign Minister Takeo Fukuda during Gromyko's first and only visit to Japan in January 1972. The Soviet leadership is said to have subsequently considered the question during preparations for the visit of Premier Kakuei Tanaka to Moscow in 1973, but supposedly rejected a revival of the two-island offer as a result of military opposition voiced through Defense Minister Andrey Grechko. (ITAR-TASS, July 29, 1992 [FBIS-SOV, July 29, 1992, p. 7].) In the fall of 1992, a KYODO news service report cited an unpublished official transcript of Gromyko's Tokyo conversations, furnished to KYODO in Moscow, as confirming that Gromyko had indeed momentarily revived the question of a two-island deal in January 1972. (KYODO (Tokyo), October 20, 1992 [FBIS-EAS, October 21, 1992, p. 6].) Japanese eyewitnesses have also long contended that Brezhnev in a weak moment told Tanaka privately that the territorial issue could be treated as an unresolved issue. The Soviets at the time and ever thereafter denied that Brezhnev had said that. It would appear that there was indeed some momentary disagreement and vacillation within the Soviet leadership on the Kurils issue, which soon vanished as détente with the United States dwindled.

[16]Personal communication to author.

Although the Soviet leadership appears to have temporarily lost interest in exploring this possibility after Andropov died and was succeeded by the Brezhnevite apparatchik Chernenko, the two-island alternative evidently resurfaced in Soviet thinking not long after Gorbachev took power. By 1987, despite the adamant Soviet public statements to the contrary, Soviet unofficial representatives behind the scenes were again taking informal soundings from Japanese opinion leaders about a two-island compromise,[17] and the following year the two-island question became a subject of overt diplomatic sparring.

In June 1988, during consultations with the Soviets in Moscow, Deputy Foreign Minister Kuriyama is reported to have told the Soviets privately that "we are against any notion of substituting the border confirmation issue for the Northern Territories issue."[18] The Japanese government appeared to fear that were it to agree to define the problem as merely one of demarcating the border between Hokkaido and the Kurils, it might be drawn into accepting a distinction between the two smallest islands adjacent to Hokkaido and the two larger ones that are further away, a distinction that would be damaging to its claim to the latter. Although the Soviets maintain that Japan signed away all rights to the Kurils at the San Francisco conference at the end of World War II, Khrushchev had suggested in 1956—as some Soviets and Russians have done since then—that Shikotan and the Habomais might be returned because these two islands, unlike the other two, were not really part of the Kurils, but were instead part of Hokkaido.

A Japanese Foreign Ministry spokesman subsequently declared that the Soviet government had not directly raised the issue of redefining the Northern Territories question in this way during Kuriyama's consultations in Moscow. However, Japan is said to have told the Soviet government that it was aware that a suggestion of this kind was being discussed "in some Soviet circles," and that Japan was taking the occasion to make it clear that it was unacceptable.[19] It would appear that Japan believed the Gorbachev leadership had encouraged Soviet

---

[17]Personal communication to author.

[18]*Asahi Shimbun,* June 28, 1988.

[19]KYODO news service, June 30, 1988.

academics to raise the notion privately as a trial balloon, while the Soviet government remained uncommitted and could disavow the notion whenever it desired.[20]   The Japanese government therefore took preemptive action to rebuff the suggestion explicitly.

The Japanese Foreign Ministry was probably particularly concerned to do this because it believed Gorbachev might raise the matter with a prominent leader of the Liberal Democratic Party (LDP), former Prime Minister Nakasone, who visited Moscow in the summer of 1988 immediately after Kuriyama.   In his talks with Nakasone, Gorbachev indeed made apparent both his interest in testing Japan's willingness to accept a two-island settlement and his reluctance to commit the Soviet Union to such a solution in the absence of good reason to believe that Japan would settle on this basis. Gorbachev is reported to have reminded Nakasone of Khrushchev's 1956 conditional offer to return the Habomais and Shikotan.   Although Gorbachev did not offer to revive Khrushchev's proposal, his readiness to discuss this precedent with Nakasone was interpreted in Japan as new evidence "that he [Gorbachev] is trying to shake Japan's firm position that all four islands must be restored to the nation."[21]

In October 1988, Yevgeniy Primakov, a Gorbachev adviser who was then director of the World Economics and International Relations Institute, visited Japan and again vaguely held out the prospect of a two-island solution. Primakov said that "some sort of positive situation may be created" provided that "Japan admits that it was not right to have rejected the terms of the [1956] Japan-USSR joint declaration"—in other words, to have declined to settle for Khrushchev's two-island offer.[22] Throughout the remainder of the Gorbachev era, the Soviet Foreign Ministry and others in and around the leadership continued to probe for revival of the two-island formula, with

---

[20]During a visit to Japan the following month, Kovalenko did precisely this, denying that any Soviet official had endorsed the notion of a two-island solution, while acknowledging that "Soviet academicians may have mentioned it." *(Mainichi Shinbum,* July 13, 1988.)

[21]*Yomiuri Shimbun,* July 24, 1988; KYODO, July 27, 1988.

[22]*Asahi Shimbun,* October 26, 1988.

uniformly negative results.[23] As will be seen, this issue was to recur prominently in the post-coup era, after Yeltsin as Russia's leader took over from Gorbachev primary responsibility for dealing with Japan.

It should be noted that the biggest difficulty—and ambiguity—of the two-island formula remains today what it was in 1988, when Gorbachev resumed Soviet maneuvering over the issue. That central problem is what, if anything, a two-island understanding would imply about the future status of the other two islands, Kunashiri (Kunashir) and Etorofu (Iturup).[24] The Japanese have traditionally insisted that the territorial issue would not be fully resolved with transfer to Japan of Shikotan and the Habomais, and that such a transfer would have to be linked in some fashion to the future disposition of Kunashiri and Etorofu. Indeed, the Japanese have always maintained that the inevitability of some such linkage was tacitly conceded by Khrushchev during the negotiations leading up to his October 1956 agreement to cede Shikotan and the Habomais. The Soviets in later years always vigorously denied that they had made any such concession, but recently Russian liberals have alleged the existence of 1956 official correspondence in which the Soviets did commit themselves to further negotiation about what they termed Kunashir and Iturup, prior to the signing of a peace treaty.[25]

---

[23]In September 1990, for example, Far East Institute director Mikhail Titarenko told a Japanese newspaper that he and his institute were convinced that Gromyko's 1960 memorandum abandoning the 1956 commitment to return two islands should now be revoked by the Soviet leadership. (Nihon Keizai Shimbun, September 5, 1990.) Almost simultaneously, Gorbachev foreign policy adviser Primakov, now a member of his Presidential Council, was said to have "suggested" to a group of visiting Japanese legislators that the Soviet Union was prepared to fulfill the 1956 commitment. (JIJI news service, Tokyo, September 7, 1990.) In late September, an unofficial draft of a proposed agreement along those lines was said to have been handed to a visiting LDP delegation. But "Japanese political circles" again indicated that a two-island solution without any commitment regarding sovereignty over the other two islands would be insufficient. Thereupon, the Soviet Foreign Ministry as usual officially denied having had anything to do with such a document. (Moscow radio, October 9, 1990 [FBIS-SOV, October 10, 1990, p. 15].)

[24]These are the Japanese and Russian versions, respectively, of the names of the two largest and most important of the disputed Northern Territories.

[25]"Not everyone knows that the 1956 Joint Declaration [between Japan and the USSR] was just one of several documents signed at that time. Before the main document was drawn up, letters were exchanged between Gromyko and [Foreign Minister] Matsumoto which defined the sides' actions in the interim period between the signing of the document and the conclusion of a peace treaty. These stipulated that any

Although the maximum Japanese position in the pre-Gorbachev period and throughout most of the Gorbachev era—when no progress was expected—had been to insist that all four islands had to be transferred simultaneously, since early 1991 Tokyo has retreated from this stance. Japan has tended increasingly to soften the linkage being demanded, deferring the eventual transfer to Japan of Kunashiri and Etorofu further into the indefinite future and rendering somewhat more abstract the commitment regarding those two islands which it was asking of Moscow. During Gorbachev's last year, Tokyo thus began to employ a formula asking that Gorbachev acknowledge in principle the "residual sovereignty" of Japan over all four islands,[26] while postponing surrender of the larger two islands. In 1992 this formula was presented once again to Yeltsin with the contention that it was an innovation. We shall return below to the implications of this issue for the future of the Russian-Japanese relationship.

GORBACHEV'S COURTSHIP OF JAPAN

With Gorbachev's conversations with Nakasone in the summer of 1988 and Shevardnadze's second visit to Tokyo five months later, the Gorbachev leadership entered a period of more aggressive courtship of Japan. Having significantly improved the Soviet relationship with America and West Europe, and having finally secured Chinese agreement to a Sino-Soviet summit, Gorbachev saw the impasse with Japan as the last major obstacle to completion of normalization of

---

agreement on the transfer of Shikotan and Habomai to Japan would be merely the first phase of a territorial settlement. The destiny of Kunashir and Iturup would be decided during the next phase, and resolution of this issue would be seen as a condition for the signing of a peace treaty. One way or another, some kind of settlement will have to be found in respect to all the islands." (Aleksandr Anichkin, "Kurils Outline: Is Agreement with Japan Possible?" *Izvestiya*, February 20, 1992 [FBIS-SOV, February 25, 1992, pp. 25–27].)

[26]The ongoing shift in the Japanese position on this point began to be reflected in the Western press by early 1991 (see *The Economist*, January 19, 1991). In February, Masashi Nishihara, professor at the National Defence Academy in Tokyo, was quoted as saying that this formula (restoring the Soviet offer to return the two smaller islands, recognizing Japanese sovereignty over the others, and agreeing to negotiate about their return) was the minimum acceptable offer Gorbachev could bring with him when he visited Tokyo in April. (*Far Eastern Economic Review*, February 21, 1991.) During the next few weeks, LDP secretary general Ichiro Ozawa apparently consolidated an official consensus behind the new formula in the course of preparations for his March 1991 visit to Moscow, discussed below.

relations with all the adversaries he had inherited from Brezhnev around the Soviet periphery. Meanwhile, as the Soviet internal economic situation had worsened, Gorbachev had become more sensitive to the importance of getting a bigger Japanese input into the Soviet economy. Although at no point subsequently did he feel it politically possible to give the Japanese the main concessions they demanded, he now sought to do what he could to secure a breakthrough without making such concessions.

To this end, he took the important step of completing the revamping of the foreign policy team that had obstructed change in Soviet strategy in the Far East. Gromyko, of course, had been pushed out of control over foreign policy at the beginning of the Gorbachev era, in the summer of 1985. In January 1987, Gorbachev had removed Deputy Foreign Minister Kapitsa, and in November 1988—shortly before he sent Shevardnadze to Tokyo for the second time—he retired Kapitsa's senior ally in the party apparatus, International Department deputy head Kovalenko.

These acts were apparently a necessary preliminary to the creation of multiple channels of dialogue with the Japanese, which followed over the next two years. Gorbachev now opened the Soviet media to occasional statements of the Japanese point of view. He made symbolic gestures such as allowing visits by Japanese to grave sites in the Northern Territories. He sent both Shevardnadze and his other close political ally, Aleksandr Yakovlev, to Tokyo to probe terms for a compromise. As already noted, during 1988 he stopped refusing to discuss the Northern Territories issue, and allowed Shevardnadze to agree that this issue would come under the purview of the new joint commission set up with the Japanese to consider the future of the relationship and the question of a bilateral peace treaty. And finally, in September 1989 he pledged to visit Japan in 1991, after refusing for four years to commit himself to a date for a visit. This public promise created a deadline that increased the political stakes the Northern Territories issue posed for both sides during the run-up to the visit.

GORBACHEV'S USE OF DÉTENTE FOR LEVERAGE ON JAPAN

At the same time, Gorbachev persistently sought to make use of the new leverage on Japan created by his improvement of relations with the United States, Western Europe, and China, suggesting to the Japanese that Tokyo was being left behind in the general movement toward détente, and that Japan should therefore consent to a comparable improvement of economic and political ties without insisting on its demands regarding the Northern Territories. Although he failed to offer concessions to Japan comparable in importance to those he had made in dealings with the Europeans, the People's Republic of China, and the United States, he sought to use this very asymmetry as an instrument to pressure Japan. His representatives constantly told the Japanese that they ran the risk of becoming isolated if they did not accept détente with the USSR on Soviet terms.

Simultaneously, Gorbachev continued to press both Japan and the United States with proposals for confidence-building measures (CBMs) and mutual naval limitations and reductions in northeast Asia. These proposals were all regarded in Japanese official circles as designed (a) to constrict or embarrass U.S.-Japanese military cooperation and (b) to obtain asymmetrical effects on the military balance in East Asia through reductions in the U.S. naval power that had traditionally offset Soviet land and air predominance in the region.

On the whole, Gorbachev's policy was both to cultivate Japan and to strive to outwait Japan, against the chance that the spread of détente elsewhere would in time sufficiently increase Soviet leverage on Tokyo. In effect, Gorbachev was hoping that the growth of Tokyo's concerns about becoming isolated would outrace the growth of his own concerns over his need for Japanese help for his deteriorating economy.

In the late 1980s, this Gorbachev strategy began to generate considerable anxiety in the Japanese Foreign Ministry about the evolving tone of the American relationship with the USSR. The Japanese government became increasingly worried about the contrast between the cool Soviet relationship with Japan and the growing enthusiasm about Gorbachev among the population of the United States and Western Europe. As Soviet-American global détente expanded, some apprehension began to emerge in Tokyo that the United States might eventually wish to enter negotiations on certain of Gorbachev's CBM proposals. In the last two years of the Reagan administration, President Reagan's summit meetings with Gorbachev—and especially the impression created by some of Mr. Reagan's more enthusiastic unplanned statements—evoked a good deal of chagrin in Tokyo. The more cautious approach toward Moscow initially adopted by the Bush administration at first eased this Japanese concern to some extent. But Gorbachev's consent in 1989 to the highly asymmetrical agreement on reduction of conventional forces in Europe, followed by his tame acceptance of Eastern Europe's revolutions and the collapse of the Warsaw Pact late that year, were milestones that greatly reinforced the Japanese Foreign Ministry's fears about being seen to be out of step with epoch-making worldwide trends. As will be seen, this problem was to return in a new form during the Yeltsin era.

THE MOBILIZATION OF THE LDP

One consequence of the anxieties thus raised in Tokyo was to begin to create strains in what hitherto had seemed a monolithic Japanese consensus. A minority of scholars and journalists began to question more vigorously the doctrine that the islands must be returned prior to the granting of Moscow's pleas for the expansion of economic investment and assistance. Instead, this minority began to urge that Japan could afford to sign a peace treaty and accept a radical improvement in political and economic relations with Moscow at the outset, in the expectation that such an improvement would eventually make the Soviet Union willing to yield the islands.

Although to this day the advocates of this view have never prevailed in Tokyo, during 1989 and 1990 they gradually began to have a modest cumulative impact on the behavior of the network of senior Liberal Democratic Party leaders, business leaders, and officials of the government bureaucracy who together constitute the Japanese governing elite. For many years, despite the hard-line position regarding the Soviet Union traditionally adhered to by the LDP, some LDP leaders had dreamed of establishing a place in history by engineering a breakthrough in relations with Moscow. In consequence, a certain underlying tension on this subject had always existed between the LDP leadership and Foreign Ministry officials because the latter saw their role in terms of reigning in ambitious politicians from unwise departures from traditional policy toward Moscow. Now, this uneasy balance was disturbed by the increasing disquiet within the

LDP over the risk of Japan's isolation from its Western partners on Soviet policy.

The net result of the more assertive role of the LDP leadership was to influence Japanese policymakers to discard insistence on recovering all four islands at once, and also to allow a slowly increasing trickle of exceptions to the dictum that the growth of the economic relationship with Moscow must wait on the satisfaction of Japan's political demands. Although the overall posture toward Moscow did not radically change, a felt need not to be seen in the West as unnecessarily intransigent eventually also led to some personnel shifts within the Foreign Ministry, as some of the most implacable ministry figures were moved out of direct responsibility for dealings with Moscow.[27]

These modest adjustments in the Foreign Ministry's policy orientation reflected, among other things, the efforts of the late former Foreign Minister Shintaro Abe, who was the key LDP politician handling Soviet policy toward the end of the 1980s. Because Abe enjoyed an unusual degree of respect among career diplomats within his ministry, he was able to steer the ministry in the direction of a more nuanced stance. Thus, for example, soon after the Houston summit meeting of the Group of Seven industrial powers in July 1990, Japanese government officials, including then-Premier Kaifu, began to articulate the concept of "expanding equilibrium" to suggest that Japan was not committed to blocking all improvement in Soviet-Japanese relations until the territorial issue was settled.

Finally, during the period immediately leading up to Gorbachev's April 1991 visit, the prospect of continued stalemate served to stimulate one senior LDP figure outside the Foreign Ministry to temporarily seize from the ministry a direct and major role in dealings with Gorbachev. This was Ichiro Ozawa, then secretary-general of the LDP, who had become the leading party politician concerned with Soviet policy after Abe became ill with cancer, and who has remained to this day the figure most prominent in attempts to revitalize Japanese policymaking and policies. Concerned over the conse-

---

[27]See Tsuyoshi Hasegawa, "Soviet-Japanese Relations in the 1990s," *Far Eastern Affairs* (Moscow), No. 2, 1991, 140–141. By 1991, a somewhat wider range of views on Soviet policy began to be evident to many visitors to the Foreign Ministry. However, the extent of this change to date should not be exaggerated.

quences if the Gorbachev visit did fail, Ozawa came to Moscow in late March for discussions with Gorbachev and other Soviet leaders, and made the most vigorous Japanese effort to date to close the gap. After months building an ephemeral consensus in the LDP, the Japanese business community, and parts of the government bureaucracy,[28] Ozawa presented Gorbachev with a package that evidently gave the Soviets the most concrete information they had ever received about the scope and nature of the economic quid pro quo they might obtain in return for surrender of the islands.[29] Accord-ing to several plausible accounts, the package proposed included:

- $4 billion worth of emergency loans to be granted quickly by the Export-Import Bank of Japan to help provide the Soviet Union with consumer goods;

- Another $4 billion to be made available for reimbursing the Soviet Union for moving its citizens off the islands, withdrawing the troops stationed there, and paying compensation for loss of property;

- Another $8 billion to be guaranteed by the Japanese government for private-sector loans, mainly for oil and gas projects in and around Sakhalin; and

---

[28]Most of the Japanese business community was not enthusiastic about investments in the Soviet Union under the conditions that prevailed there in the spring of 1991, but Japanese business leaders were apparently temporarily won over by Ozawa's argument that a decisive Japanese commitment for the sake of a settlement would pay long-term dividends. Meanwhile, endorsement of the Ozawa package was weakest in the third section of the traditional Japanese elite triumvirate, the government bureaucracy, which was apparently divided over the issue. Many Japanese observers believe that Ozawa had worked with officials of the Ministry for International Trade and Investment (MITI) to prepare the package. Some suggest that Ozawa simply used MITI support to override Foreign Ministry opposition, while others believe that some senior Foreign Ministry officials temporarily acquiesced but disowned the project after it had failed. (I am indebted to Mike Mochizuki for insights regarding this internal struggle in the Japanese governing elite.)

[29]As already suggested, the Japanese bargaining tactic of declining to become specific about this quid pro quo in the absence of a preliminary Soviet commitment to Japanese demands had certainly been one of the reasons for the impasse. The previous fall, *Argumenty i Fakty* editor Aleksey Surkov, who was inclined to be conciliatory, expressed impatience with this reticence and told a Japanese newspaper that "no progress will be made" until Japan gave the USSR "a clear-cut guarantee about what it plans to give the Soviet Union in return for the four islands." *(Sankei Shimbun* (Tokyo), September 4, 1990.)

- $10 billion for general Soviet economic development to be lent at low interest rates to help build factories and roads and develop natural resources.[30]

Meanwhile, regarding the other side of the proposed bargain, Ozawa was prepared to convey to Gorbachev the new, more flexible Japanese position on transfer of the disputed territories: namely, that all four islands did not have to be returned simultaneously, that it would suffice to return Habomais and Shikotan initially and to defer the return of Etorofu and Kunashiri for a long time, provided that Gorbachev was willing to adopt some formula at the outset acknowledging Japanese sovereignty in principle over all four islands.[31] In addition, Japan would promise not to deploy military forces to the islands and was ready to offer special economic assistance to Sakhalin and to grant permanent residence to Soviet residents of the islands who wanted to remain.[32]

REASONS FOR THE GORBACHEV SUMMIT FAILURE

From the perspective of the Gorbachev leadership, these proposals had the virtue of making much clearer than before the terms of the

---

[30] *Yomiuri Shimbun,* March 21, 1991; *The Economist,* March 30, 1991, p. 33. The Ozawa package proposal was conveyed to Gorbachev a few days in advance of the Ozawa visit, and its existence was leaked by a Gorbachev subordinate on March 20. Some Japanese reports alluded to the package as worth $28 billion rather than $26 billion. Details of the offer were never officially confirmed, and Japanese Foreign Minister Taro Nakayama professed to know nothing about it. (JIJI press agency, Tokyo, March 28, 1991.) After the offer was rejected, the ministry was particularly eager to treat it as a non-event. But although in consequence some Washington observers still regard the Ozawa offer as unconfirmed, there seems little doubt that it was made and that it was substantially as described above. Indeed, Japanese diplomats today privately acknowledge the fact of the offer, while simultaneously treating it as an aberration that must never be repeated.

[31] As earlier suggested, Ozawa evidently secured the backing of the Japanese elite consensus for this position in the course of putting together support for his economic package. During the week before Ozawa left for Moscow, the new doctrine was publicly endorsed first by Gaishi Hiraiwa, chairman of the Federation of Economic Organizations (Keidanren), and then by Ozawa himself. A "Foreign Ministry source" then confirmed the shift, although not for personal attribution. (KYODO, March 19 and 22, 1991; also, *The Wall Street Journal,* March 25, 1991.)

[32] Shortly before Ozawa left for Moscow, his LDP associate Koko Sato journeyed to Sakhalin and conveyed these additional particulars to local Soviet leaders. (KYODO news service, March 19, 1991.)

bargain Moscow was being asked to consider. Gorbachev could at least congratulate himself that his efforts to lever Japan with the threat of isolation from the general trend toward world détente had had sufficient effect to compel the Japanese elite to put its cards on the table. To do this, the Japanese political leadership had been compelled to take the initiative away from Foreign Ministry officials who were reluctant to abandon the negotiating practice of avoiding any specific commitment in advance of a Soviet commitment. The Foreign Ministry has remained unhappy at this aberration and has since worked successfully within the Japanese elite to ensure that it not be repeated.

On the other hand, from Gorbachev's perspective the Ozawa proposals, while much clearer than before, had one fatal flaw: they came too late. They were presented at a time when Gorbachev's political capability to accept any such package had drastically deteriorated because of the internal trend of events in the Soviet Union.

For the very reason that the Japanese economic offer was now more specific, it could be more easily attacked behind the scenes in Moscow as an inadequate quid pro quo. It is likely, for example, that objectors stressed the fact that no Japanese outright grants were envisioned, but only loans, many of which could be portrayed by Soviet opponents as intended to serve Japanese rather than Soviet economic interests in exploiting Soviet resources. Others may also have contended that the Ozawa package, despite its scope, was still incommensurate with what Moscow was being asked to give up.

In point of fact, however, almost any Japanese offer would have been foredoomed by the domestic circumstances that now surrounded Gorbachev. When Gorbachev arrived in Tokyo in April 1991, he was weaker at home than he had ever been before. The loss of Eastern Europe, the collapse of the Warsaw Pact, the growing economic disaster, and the centrifugal process that was tearing the Soviet Union apart had united in response a coalition of military and civilian reactionaries infuriated over what was happening and longing to turn back the clock. In the winter of 1990–1991 Gorbachev had temporarily capitulated to massive pressure from the leaders of the military and security forces, and had consented to an attempted crackdown to try to halt the disintegration of the country. In the process, he had betrayed and jettisoned his two key reformist allies, Shevardnadze and Yakovlev—the two men, incidentally, who had also played the leading roles up to then in attempting to find a compromise with Japan.

As a by-product, the military and KGB leaders had become much bolder in expressing their views on a wide variety of subjects, and Minister of Defense Dmitriy Yazov had gratuitously volunteered a denunciation of the notion that the islands claimed by Japan could ever be sacrificed for any consideration.[33] A good measure of the impact of military opinion on Soviet policy in the Far East in this period was Gorbachev's continued inability to secure the opening of Vladivostok in the face of strenuous naval opposition, despite his repeated promises to do so and public demands by Shevardnadze that it be done.[34] In the meantime, the continued growth of the role of the Soviet republics at the expense of Gorbachev's all-union center had created yet another obstacle to any accord with Japan, since Yeltsin and the leaders of the Russian republic, intent on expanding their authority at Gorbachev's expense, now insisted that no agreement was possible without their appoval.

To be sure, Gorbachev's swing to the right was not permanent. Immediately after his April 1991 trip to Japan, he was to turn away from his alliance with the military-industrial complex to meet and seek an understanding with Yeltsin and eight other republic leaders. But Gorbachev's personal position remained extremely weak, and continued to deteriorate in the face of pressures from both right and left until his disgusted former allies in the Ministry of Defense and the KGB launched the coup attempt of August 1991.

In retrospect, the last moment when Gorbachev may have had the political strength to force through acceptance of the deal Ozawa proposed in 1991 was probably some time in the first half of 1989, before

---

[33]*Mainichi Shimbun,* December 20, 1990.

[34]In a September 1990 address to the USSR Supreme Soviet, Shevardnadze had publicly insisted that "it is necessary to do away with the 'closed' status of Vladivostok without delay." (TASS, September 11, 1990.) This did not happen, however, until power had passed to Yeltsin with the failure of the August 1991 coup. A month after the coup, Yeltsin finally issued a decree announcing that the city would be opened on January 1, 1992. The Russian press then noted that the USSR Ministry of Defense had continued to oppose this step up to the last minute. *(Komsomolskaya Pravda,* September 25, 1991.)

the fall of Eastern Europe. But at that time Gorbachev himself was probably not yet ready to pay the personal political price involved in acknowledging even "residual" Japanese sovereignty over all four of the Northern Territories. Nor was Gorbachev yet prepared to assign top priority to a settlement with Japan, since he was preoccupied at the time with coping with domestic resistance to the enormous concessions he was about to make to NATO to secure agreement on reduction of conventional forces in Europe. Nor, for their part, were the Japanese themselves prepared in 1989 to offer Gorbachev a detailed package comparable in scope to the one Ozawa carried to Moscow in 1991. Thus both sides proved in the end to be behind the curve of history.

For these reasons, Gorbachev's April 1991 visit to Tokyo could not and did not resolve the impasse. After his cold reception of the Ozawa offer that had been put together with such difficulty and brought to Moscow in March, the reaction within the Japanese governing elite was severe. Meanwhile, despite continued hints that Gorbachev would welcome a return to Khrushchev's 1956 two-island formula,[35] Gorbachev did not explicitly commit himself even to that solution, if only because it was apparent that Japan would not accept the formula without some additional commitment in principle regarding the other two islands. Instead, Gorbachev acknowledged that he no longer considered Japan's territorial claims to be a non-issue, repeating a tactical concession which the USSR had implied long before and had formally announced the previous September. He also announced Soviet intention to make some reductions in the forces deployed in the Northern Territories, a conciliatory gesture that was helpful but far from sufficient. The two sides took the occasion of the visit to firm up mechanisms to continue the dialogue, and both governments sought to put the best face on the results. But both were well aware that a settlement would have to await further events in the Soviet Union.

---

[35]In March, Gorbachev's presidential spokesman Vitaliy Ignatenko told a Japanese newspaper that the Kremlin was "studying" the 1956 Japan-Soviet Joint Declaration. (*Asahi Evening News*, March 16, 1991.)

Chapter Three

YELTSIN AND THE DECLINE OF POST-COUP HOPES

EXPECTATIONS AND CONSTRAINING REALITIES

In the aftermath of the collapse of the August 1991 Moscow coup, expectations were voiced in many quarters that conditions had now become much more favorable for a settlement of the Kuril dispute and for a breakthrough in relations between Moscow and Tokyo.[1] The new wave of hope was propelled by three considerations.

- First, and above all, there was the general belief that there had been a major shift in the balance of Soviet political power as a result of the failure of the coup. The political leverage of the Soviet military and their reactionary civilian allies had evidently been significantly diminished, and with it—so it was then supposed— had gone the General Staff's ability to obstruct prospective territorial concessions to Japan.

- Second, from the moment of the collapse of the coup, the decisive role in all aspects of policy in Moscow—including policy toward Japan—began to pass from the fading Soviet center to the Russian republic and its leader Boris Yeltsin, a change that was completed and formalized four months later with the demise of

---

[1]Typical was a comment of an unidentified Japanese Foreign Ministry official seven weeks after the coup attempt: "On the territorial issue, there is no real change. . . . But our whole relationship has changed. . .since the collapse of the putsch. . . . With the conservative forces defeated, there are now possibilities, chances and hopes we did not have before. Those give grounds for optimism." *(Los Angeles Times,* October 17, 1991.)

the Soviet state and Gorbachev's disappearance from the political stage. Many observers assumed that the replacement of the weak and vacillating Gorbachev at the heart of the policy formulation process by the radical and apparently more forthright Yeltsin, the hero who had defeated the coup, would at last make possible decisive steps to close the gap with Japan.

• Finally, it was widely assumed that the increasingly desperate economic crisis in Russia would make its leaders more aware of their need to propitiate Japan, which had the largest available pool of capital that might be made available to assist the former Soviet republics.

Although all these assumptions had some validity, they failed to take into account other factors that over the next year were to create imposing new barriers to a Russian-Japanese settlement.

The first consideration was the fact that Boris Yeltsin, despite his record as the radical standard-bearer of democracy and reform, was also a politician who was acutely sensitive to the interplay of political pressures around him and who was convinced of the need to set priorities in accepting political risks and in spending his political capital. As will be seen, even before he replaced Gorbachev, this felt need for caution had always conditioned Yeltsin's behavior toward the Japanese territorial demands.

Moreover, once he took power, Yeltsin's domestic political strength, so imposing at first, was necessarily a gradually diminishing asset. The longer the economic crisis went on, and the more painful the consequences of his attempts to move toward a market economy, the more vulnerable he would become, and the more difficult it would therefore be to make big concessions to Japan. To make progress on his overall agenda he would have to accept grave risks on not one but many fronts, and even he could not face the consequences of attempting to do so everywhere.

Thus, for example, he could not avoid the political dangers involved in freeing prices and allowing them to rise, with all the suffering this caused. Nor, if he were to make a serious effort to hold down growth of the budget deficit and avoid hyperinflation, could he indefinitely avoid facing the political consequences of reducing traditional subsidies for many unprofitable factories and thereby allowing thou-

sands of workers to lose their jobs. Nor, since he desperately needed
to make drastic cuts in military expenditures, did he feel he could
avoid making extraordinary and unprecedented concessions to the
United States in a nuclear arms agreement that greatly displeased
many of his military advisers. Each of these steps represented a major calculated risk, an additional new drain on his political capital,
and each necessarily had a higher priority than major concessions to
Japan.   Since the scale of expenditures of political capital which
Yeltsin could afford to make was limited, big concessions to Japan
were rapidly squeezed off the agenda.

In addition, Yeltsin was forced to deal with the emotional consequences of the collapse of what had really been a Russian empire.
The dissolution of the Soviet Union meant the end of long-established Russian control over many nations adjacent to Russia in the
borderlands of the former Soviet Union, from the Baltics in the north
to the Caucasus in the south. Particularly traumatic for almost all
Russians was the end of many centuries of close association with
Ukraine. One consequence of all this pain and humiliation was the
rapid growth of a Russian nationalist/chauvinist trend in Moscow,
which came to embrace not only the old right wing but also broad
sectors of the old democratic and reformist movement. Meanwhile,
at several points around the Russian periphery (Moldova, Ossetia,
the Baltics, as well as the southern Kurils) local intransigents looking
to Russia for protection found powerful backing from the increasingly nationalistic tendency in Moscow. The common denominator
has been a certain aggressiveness about defending Russians outside
Russia, particularly when their local opponents are sufficiently weak,
coupled with an emotional inflexibility about further retreat from
territory anywhere around the Russian periphery. The combination,
although not all-powerful, has produced visible leverage on much of
Yeltsin's behavior, including his behavior toward Japan on the Kurils
issue.

YELTSIN'S FIVE STAGES

Yeltsin's policy on the Northern Territories issue since he took power
is still anchored in the most explicit and detailed statement he has
made to date on the subject, the position he unveiled during a visit to

Japan in January 1990, long before his victory over Gorbachev. At that time, Yeltsin proposed a lengthy sequence of five stages.

In the first stage, the Soviet Union would "officially and clearly" acknowledge the existence of the territorial issue in Soviet-Japanese relations. (As earlier noted, at the time Yeltsin issued his five-point plan Gorbachev had implied that he accepted that there was a valid territorial issue, but had not yet publicly and explicitly said so.) Yeltsin noted that this step should be taken when Gorbachev visited Japan, as indeed happened. Yeltsin insisted that such outright acknowledgment was not a mere formality but was politically important because it was a prerequisite for preparing Soviet public opinion to consider calmly the historical background of the issue.

In a second stage, the four islands would be declared a "free enterprise zone" open to Japan. Yeltsin did not fully clarify the characteristics of this zone, but he apparently envisaged a status that would allow and encourage the growth of major Japanese local investment—a process which, in turn, over time, might help to transform local attitudes. He thought this stage would take three to four years. In some later versions of his plan, he said that not just the four disputed islands, but all of Sakhalin oblast (of which the islands were a part) should become a free economic zone.

In the third stage, the islands would be demilitarized. Because, as he said sarcastically, "the islands belong to our military rather than to our state," Yeltsin in January 1990 thought this might take as long as five to seven years. As will be seen, after taking power he greatly shortened this estimate.

In the fourth stage, after perhaps another five years, the Soviet Union and Japan would sign a peace treaty. Yeltsin called on Japan to make "a half step forward," and to become willing to sign the treaty before return of the islands.

Finally, after these four preliminary stages comprising a total of some 15–20 years, a new generation would find some "original, unorthodox" solution for the territorial question. Yeltsin refused to pin himself down as to the nature of the territorial settlement that would eventually emerge, but did suggest three hypothetical alternatives:

the creation of a joint Soviet-Japanese protectorate over the islands, granting them independence, or transferring them to Japan.[2]

It should be noted that Yeltsin's plan, as enunciated and repeated, did not embody a return to Khrushchev's 1956 two-island offer regarding Shikotan and the Habomais (although, as we shall see, the Russian Foreign Ministry continued to toy with that idea). Nevertheless, if this Yeltsin package had provided for an explicit Soviet pledge at the outset of the process for *eventual* full reversion of the four islands to Japan (no matter how much delayed), it would have gone a long way toward meeting Japanese concerns. But Yeltsin, like Gorbachev, was unwilling to do this. Consequently, his package has remained unacceptable to the Japanese leadership.

To date, Yeltsin has never ventured, in any personal public statement, much beyond the framework of his five-stage plan, although after coming to power in 1991 he was to suggest that the time required might be significantly reduced.

COMPETITIVE DEMAGOGUERY

After Yeltsin launched his five-stage idea in January 1990, he began to show increasing caution on the Kurils territorial issue, and as his political stature as Gorbachev's principal rival grew he went to increasing lengths to propitiate Russian nationalist opinion. In August 1990, now Chairman of the Russian Supreme Soviet, Yeltsin visited Sakhalin and the Kurils and was at pains to reassure local inhabitants that his plan did not envisage any "handover" to the Japanese.[3] Beginning in the fall of 1990, as the Soviet Foreign Ministry intensified negotiations with Japan over the coming Gorbachev visit, Yeltsin and his followers began to seize on the issue as a vehicle in the internal struggle for power. In October, Russian Foreign Minister Andrey Kozyrev said that a solution of the territorial dispute would be impossible unless the Russian republic were involved along with

---

[2]Summary of Yeltsin speech to Japan Society of Asian Studies, January 16, 1990 (*Mainichi Shimbun*, January 17, 1990). This is the fullest available version of Yeltsin's presentation of his five-stage program while he was in Japan. See also his subsequent interview in *New Times* (Moscow), No. 6, February 6–12, 1990.

[3]Moscow radio interview, August 22, 1990 (FBIS-SOV, August 23, 1990, p. 80).

Gorbachev in the negotiations with the Japanese. In November, Yeltsin said that the Russian Federation would take no responsibility for any international commitments unless it had been consulted beforehand. A Declaration of Sovereignty adopted by the Russian parliament gave the Japanese warning that these statements could have practical consequences, stipulating that any change in Russian territory must be authorized through a referendum of the Russian people.

In January 1991, Yeltsin went so far as to tell a visiting Japanese parliamentary delegation that Russia could conclude a "peace treaty" with Japan "without waiting for the [Japanese] completion of one with the union."[4] The Japanese were not likely to be impressed, however. They were certainly not prepared at that stage to embarrass their negotiations with Gorbachev by signing any such document with the Russian Federation. Even more important, as Yeltsin well knew, Japan was in any case unwilling to sign a peace treaty with *anyone* in the Soviet Union without some acknowledgment of Japanese sovereignty over all four islands, and Yeltsin and his supporters made it amply clear that they were no more willing to do this than was Gorbachev. Very much to the contrary: during late 1990 and early 1991 Yeltsin and his followers, for reasons having nothing to do with Japan, did their best to create a climate of opinion that would make it even more difficult for Gorbachev to make significant concessions to Japan in return for economic benefits.

"It is inconceivable," Yeltsin said in a French television interview, "that we would sell the Kurils, *for whatever sum*, as we once did Alaska."[5] (Emphasis added.) One Yeltsin supporter, the millionaire Artem Tarasov, created a sensation in early 1991 by publicly asserting that Gorbachev in preparation for his April 1991 visit had worked out a secret deal with the Japanese to "sell" the Kurils for some 200 billion dollars.[6] Gorbachev was forced to deny this highly implausible allegation indignantly and to charge Tarasov with

---

[4]Moscow radio, January 9, 1991. This was not a new Yeltsin suggestion; as early as May 1990 he had begun to suggest publicly that Russia could sign a treaty with Japan independently of the USSR. (*Asahi Shimbun*, May 16, 1990.) As the Gorbachev visit to Japan grew closer, however, such disingenuous proposals naturally attracted increasing attention.

[5]*Los Angeles Times*, August 27, 1991, citing a Yeltsin statement late in 1990.

[6]*Baltimore Sun*, January 29, 1991.

slander. The tumult went on for weeks, and although Tarasov eventually withdrew his accusation, the net result was henceforth to make any attempted deal with the Japanese even more vulnerable to the insinuation that the islands were being treacherously "sold." It seems unlikely that Yeltsin was not consulted before the Tarasov maneuver. Shortly thereafter, in a speech in Kaliningrad, Yeltsin insisted that Russia would never give up an inch of its land, and gratuitously mentioned the Kurils in this connection.[7]

Subsequently, on the eve of Gorbachev's April 1991 arrival in Japan, Yeltsin pointedly reiterated that "it is inconceivable that we would sell the Kurils for whatever sum."[8] For understandable reasons, this line of Yeltsin rhetoric was not halted during his subsequent campaign for the Russian presidency, when he continued to appeal strongly to Russian nationalist sentiment in terms which seemed to rule out territorial concessions to anyone. On June 12, on the eve of the voting for the presidency, he responded to a question about the Kurils by saying that "reconsidering the borders now is out of the question; it would be blood again."[9]

In short, from the fall of 1990 until the turning point, a year later, when Yeltsin was finally able to assume responsibility for Japan policy as a result of the failure of the August coup, his statements on the subject had little to do with his policy preferences and everything to do with posturing to meet the needs of his struggle against Gorbachev. The Japanese were not favorably impressed by this behavior, although they understood the reasons for it. Yeltsin's perceived freedom to be irresponsible came to an end, however, with his assumption of power.

---

[7]KYODO news service, Tokyo, February 9, 1991 (FBIS-SOV, February 13, 1991, p. 66). See also *Rabochaya Gazeta*, February 13, 1991. Yeltsin's remarks in Kaliningrad oblast were mainly devoted to assuring the locals that he would never allow Kaliningrad to be surrendered by Russia. The Kurils were mentioned only in passing, but the next day, the Japanese embassy is reported to have bombarded the Russian Foreign Ministry with queries as to whether this meant that Yeltsin had abandoned his five-stage formula. *(Komsomolskaya Pravda,* April 25, 1991.)

[8]*Asahi Evening News*, April 9, 1991, cited by *The Wall Street Journal*, April 19–20, 1991.

[9]Western news agencies, June 12, 1991, cited in Radio Free Europe/Radio Liberty (RFE/RL) Daily Report, Sovset computer bulletin No. 111, June 13, 1991.

THE POST-COUP PROBES: KHASBULATOV AND KUNADZE

The first hint that accession to power might lead Yeltsin to adopt a more conciliatory policy toward Japan came with two trips taken by Russian officials in the first few weeks after the failed coup. One was the mission to Japan in early September led by acting Russian Supreme Soviet chairman Ruslan Khasbulatov (who subsequently became a Yeltsin adversary, but who was then still a Yeltsin ally), and the second was the journey to the Kurils undertaken soon afterward by Russian Deputy Foreign Minister Georgiy Kunadze, who had accompanied Khasbulatov to Tokyo and who had been put in charge of the Japan problem in the ministry.

The Khasbulatov mission evidently had three purposes. Above all, it was intended to make it unmistakably clear to the reluctant Japanese that the Russian government, and not Gorbachev, now at last had the power and would determine policy in any negotiations. To this end, Khasbulatov carried a letter from Yeltsin to the Japanese premier, and his companion Kunadze undoubtedly emphasized to the Japanese Foreign Ministry that the Soviet Foreign Ministry would henceforth be obliged to delegate all negotiations with Japan to the Russian Foreign Ministry, that is, to him. This shift in responsibility was duly confirmed when the Japanese foreign minister visited Moscow five weeks later, and Kunadze was indeed named to deal with Japan on a bilateral working group devoted to the territorial issue.

Second, Khasbulatov came to Tokyo to place before the Japanese the Russian government's desires regarding economic aid sought from Japan, to assess the Japanese attitude on this score, and thus to evaluate the kind of quid pro quo that might be obtained for territorial concessions. He later revealed that he had asked for some $8–15 billion in emergency assistance at the outset.[10] We will consider the Japanese response below.

---

[10]TASS, September 13, 1991. In a subsequent interview, Khasbulatov emphasized that "we would like the Japanese to set an example. . . . That is why, although it was unpleasant, I had to speak of large-scale economic aid from the Japanese state, public, and business world." (*Rossiyskaya Gazeta*, September 18, 1991.)

And third, Khasbulatov was now authorized to indicate, both publicly and privately, that it might be possible to shorten the 15–20 year
period Yeltsin had suggested might be required to solve the territorial
problem under his phased approach. Khasbulatov did not state how
much time would in fact be needed, nor did he suggest that Yeltsin
was abandoning the five-stage formula or that he was prepared to
accept the Japanese demand for preliminary acknowledgment of
Japanese sovereignty over all four islands as a prerequisite for a
peace treaty. But Khasbulatov emphasized that the Yeltsin government was renouncing the assumption—which he implied had been
the past thinking of the Soviet government—that the territorial issue
was governed by the relations between victors and vanquished (i.e.,
that the Soviet Union held the islands by right of conquest).[11] And
while remaining studiously vague about details, he indicated that the
Russian government was prepared to try more vigorously to persuade
Russian public opinion to accept a compromise. He hinted that
significant progress might be made if the Japanese economic response were sufficiently forthcoming.[12]

One indication of the thinking in the Russian Foreign Ministry at this
point was provided soon thereafter by Valeriy Zaytsev, an academic
adviser to the ministry. Zaytsev told a Japanese newspaper that the
ministry was "leaning" toward taking the 1956 joint communiqué as
the starting point and returning the islands in two stages, with the
second conditional on the consequences of the first but following
fairly soon thereafter. Zaytsev was quoted as saying that

> if there is a willingness on the Japanese side to take advantage of the
> present favorable situation since the Soviet coup d'état, the return
> of Habomai and Shikotan could be accomplished in three years at
> the latest, and the return of all the islands by 1995.[13]

---

[11] *Komsomolskaya Pravda,* September 14, 1991.

[12] "Russian public opinion," he said, "is old and conservative and opposes giving the
islands to Japan. . .so Japan and Russia have to cooperate together to change the
stereotype of the people." (*Washington Times,* September 13, 1991.)

[13] Interview with Valeriy Zaytsev, director of the Japan and Pacific Area Reseach Center
of World Economics and International Relations Institute (IMEMO), *Tokyo Shimbun,*
October 3, 1991.

According to Zaytsev, the return of the Habomais and Shikotan in the first stage would serve as a "model" that would enable the Russian government to evaluate the subsequent Japanese economic response toward Russia generally, and also to assess the compensation Japan furnished to inhabitants of the islands. He claimed that if the Japanese response to the return of the first two islands was sufficient, opposition among the inhabitants of Kunashiri and Etorofu would also lessen.

This formula, if accepted by Yeltsin, would have meant collapsing his five stages drastically, and accepting personal responsibility for returning at least Shikotan and the Habomais fairly soon instead of deferring the fate of all four islands to some other Russian leadership in the distant future. For that reason, and also because this plan for the first time would have offered Japan at least conditional hopes for the return of Kunashiri and Etorofu, the proposal Zaytsev said was under consideration would have been more forthcoming than anything Moscow had heretofore put forward. This scheme still fell considerably short of meeting Japan's request for some kind of explicit advance commitment on sovereignty over Kunashiri and Etorofu. Yet it was sufficiently radical from the Russian perspective to present grave political dangers for Yeltsin and make his acceptance uncertain under the best of circumstances. In any case, however, the scheme soon became moot, because events quickly multiplied its political costs for Yeltsin and made them unacceptable to him.

Soon after returning home from Japan with Khasbulatov, Deputy Foreign Minister Kunadze undertook a September trip to Sakhalin and the Kurils. This journey was apparently intended to begin the Russian government's effort—promised by Khasbulatov—to try to persuade public opinion to look more favorably on a deal with Japan.[14] The outcome was disastrous.

---

[14]To the same end, the Russian Foreign Ministry about this time unearthed from its archives and leaked to the liberal Moscow press a document containing instructions Tsar Nicholas I had issued to his representatives when they were negotiating with the Japanese in 1853, ordering the acceptance of a Russia-Japan boundary between those islands today called the Northern Territories and the islands north of them. Thus Yeltsin's Foreign Ministry had begun to try to make the Russian population aware that there were arguments supporting the Japanese case.

FEDOROV AND THE NATIONALIST OPPOSITION

Although reliable detailed accounts of what Kunadze said in the Kurils are lacking, it seems clear that he asserted, among other things, that he was there "to tell the Kuril residents the truth about the 'Northern Territories' problem,"[15] that the truth had thus far been "rearranged in a tendentious interpretation," that "the question of territorial ownership of these islands exists. . .as an objective legal reality and. . .it is necessary to resolve it,"[16] that a solution should be "accelerated,"[17] and that in negotiations with Japan he would be guided by the 1956 Soviet-Japanese joint declaration.[18]

In response, Valentin Fedorov, head of the local government for Sakhalin and the Kurils,[19] seized the occasion to launch a vehement political offensive against negotiations of any kind with Japan over the territorial issue. This offensive, which has gone on to the present day, has achieved an importance that greatly transcends the limits of Fedorov's own political role in Russia.

Fedorov, an economist and former researcher in Moscow, had gone to Sakhalin in 1990 to take control of the local government as an economic reformer and avowed ally of Yeltsin. At the outset, his efforts to galvanize the local economy showed some promise, but as the difficulties of effecting change mounted, he became increasingly interested in exploiting nationalist passions as a vehicle for political self-promotion. Always an opponent of surrendering any of the Northern Territories to Japan, Fedorov became more outspoken in 1991 on every occasion when negotiations became active. When Ozawa carried his offer of $26 billion to Moscow in March 1991, Fedorov was stimulated to insist that *any* settlement that surrendered *any* of the islands would be treason.[20] Named a member of the delegation accompa-

---

[15]TASS, September 28, 1991.

[16]Moscow television, October 8, 1991 (FBIS-SOV, October 21, 1991, p. 17).

[17]*Rabochaya Gazeta,* October 2, 1991 (FBIS-SOV, November 1, 1991, p. 62).

[18]*Komsomolskaya Pravda,* October 2, 1991.

[19]Technically, Fedorov was chairman of the Executive Committee of the Sakhalin Oblast Soviet. Like some others in comparable positions, he had begun referring to himself as "Governor" of Sakhalin, using prevolutionary nomenclature.

[20]*Moscow News,* April 14–21, 1991.

nying Gorbachev to Tokyo the next month, Fedorov returned home early, lamenting Gorbachev's acknowledgment that the status of the four islands was a real issue, and objecting even to Gorbachev's token concessions to the Japanese (his promise to reduce forces on the islands, and his consent to allow Japanese to visit certain of the islands without visas).[21]

Now, in the fall of 1991, Fedorov called Kunadze's visit to the Kurils "the beginning of a large-scale campaign to prepare public opinion for a return of the islands to Japan."[22]   Denouncing Kunadze as a traitor who had adopted "the most unadulterated Japanese positions," Fedorov mocked him as a non-Russian who had no right to surrender Russian territory,[23] and sent telegrams to Yeltsin demanding his removal. Fedorov organized protest rallies in Sakhalin, publicly brandished the threat of a separatist movement to create a Far Eastern republic, gave numerous interviews on Moscow television, and peppered the Moscow press with articles and letters reiterating his viewpoint. In the process, he broadened the assault from Kunadze to the Russian Foreign Ministry generally, insisting that Foreign Minister Kozyrev was a person who could not be trusted. He did not attack Yeltsin directly, but repeatedly invited Yeltsin to withdraw support from Kozyrev and Kunadze.

What made all this activity worrisome to Yeltsin was that Fedorov soon gained support outside the Far East, at first from the extreme right but to some extent from others. Conservative Moscow newspapers such as *Pravda* and *Sovetskaya Rossiya* joined in Fedorov's attack on Kunadze and the Foreign Ministry, finding this a convenient point of attack on Yeltsin's administration. At Fedorov's invitation, Sergey Baburin, a prominent leader of the ultra-nationalist tendency

---

[21]POSTFACTUM News Review, April 21, 1991.

[22]TASS, October 4, 1991.

[23]Fedorov told an interviewer that "the person called Georgiy Fredrikhovich Kunadze has absolutely no moral or ethical right to decide the fate of an ages-old Russian territory." (Moscow television, October 8, 1991; *Komsomolskaya Pravda*, October 2, 1991.) This ethnic slur—an allusion to Kunadze's Georgian name—received a good deal of notoriety.

in the parliament,[24] came to Sakhalin to tour the Kurils in early October, afterward strongly praising Fedorov and asserting that surrender of any of the Kurils would endanger Russia's military security.[25] On the opposite side of Russia from the Kurils, in distant Kaliningrad, where some feared an analogous threat of eventual annexation by Germany, the local leadership voiced support for Fedorov's resistance to territorial concessions in the Kurils.[26] The nationalist pressure on Yeltsin was symbolized and considerably augmented by publication of a joint letter to him signed by many senior scientists from throughout Russia insisting that "it is inadmissable even to raise" the question of "the 'sale' of the southern Kurils."[27] And eventually, as will be seen below, the military rejoined this overt opposition to any Kurils deal.

Under these circumstances, Yeltsin began once more to dodge and equivocate, declining to support Kunadze and Kozyrev while nevertheless leaving the door ajar for negotiations with the Japanese. At a private meeting with spokesmen of all Russia's parliamentary parties, Yeltsin—according to Baburin—censured the results of Kunadze's trip to the Kurils and said he now understood the situation.[28] At about the same time, in an interview with Japanese and Russian television correspondents, Yeltsin introduced a telling quibble into his public position, denying that he had put forward a five-step plan "for a solution" of the territorial issue, and insisting that his plan provided only for "negotiations" on the issue.[29] At a subsequent private meeting with Fedorov, Yeltsin (according to Fedorov) stated that he had not authorized anyone to speak about the Kurils issue on his behalf.[30]

---

[24]Baburin had, for example, denounced a recent Russian-American agreement dividing overlapping coastal waters between Alaska and Siberia, claiming that Kozyrev had irresponsibly given away Russian maritime territory.

[25]*Sovetskaya Rossiya*, October 17, 1991; *Rabochaya Tribuna*, October 23, 1991.

[26]Kaliningrad Maritime Press Service, October 17, 1991 (FBIS-SOV, October 23, 1991).

[27]*Sovetskaya Rossiya*, October 5, 1991.

[28]INTERFAX, October 17, 1991 (FBIS-SOV, October 18, 1991, p. 68).

[29]Tokyo NHK television, October 17, 1991 (FBIS-SOV, October 18, 1991, p. 68).

[30]INTERFAX, November 4, 1991 (FBIS-SOV, November 5, 1991, p. 60).

Finally, in mid-November, Yeltsin published an open letter to the Russian people responding to the messages and protests he had received on the Kurils question. In this carefully crafted and studiously ambiguous document, Yeltsin stressed the importance of unfreezing relations with Japan, noted that the "main obstacle" to a treaty with Japan was "the question of border demarcation," said he would be guided "by the principles of justice and humanity," but pledged to "firmly defend" the interests of Russia and especially the interests of the Kuril inhabitants.[31] Thus he appeased the immediate storm without explicitly ruling out the possibility of eventual territorial concessions.

Nevertheless, the practical likelihood of any early territorial deal—much less the chance of putting into effect the radical Foreign Ministry scheme outlined by Zaytsev—had been dealt a grave blow. Over the next year, the forces working against an agreement were to grow, and the chances of reaching an understanding became more and more problematical. In retrospect, the best opportunity for a settlement may have existed briefly at the very outset, in the first month after the coup attempt, when Yeltsin's moral and political authority over factors such as the military and the Russian legislature was at its peak. As had happened before with Gorbachev, the negotiating machinery on both sides could not become engaged quickly enough, and after September 1991 the brief political window of opportunity was closed.

JAPAN, THE WEST, AND THE QUESTION OF AID TO RUSSIA

Meanwhile, Japan's diplomatic struggle with Moscow over the Northern Territories became increasingly intertwined with a struggle among the Western industrialized states over what—and how much—should be done to render economic assistance to Moscow. Bit by bit during 1991 and 1992, Japan was propelled by Western pressure—and by Tokyo's fear of becoming isolated—into reluctantly agreeing to participate in the international rescue operation that eventually emerged. To the degree that Japan yielded to these demands, it was forced to cede in advance part of the economic quid

---

[31] *Rossiyskaya Gazeta*, November 19, 1991.

pro quo it had sought to withhold from Russia pending return of the Northern Territories.

Japanese leaders are by no means oblivious to the urgent Western arguments for helping Yeltsin, nor to the costs that may ultimately be paid by all if the painful effort to transform Russia is allowed to collapse for lack of sufficient Western support. But both economic and political considerations have rendered Japan particularly reluctant to make commitments on this subject.

On the economic side, most Japanese business and government leaders have shared the view of Western skeptics that a large-scale aid effort for Russia would be wasted, and that no amount of external help would stabilize the political and economic situation in Russia. At the same time, the business community has on the whole not been interested enough in trade and investment opportunities in Russia to be motivated to exert strong pressure on the government to change course. Indeed, many business leaders, faced by the shortage of Russian infrastructure in many areas and what they see as a discouraging political and economic environment for profitable investment, apparently have been privately relieved that the Foreign Ministry's recalcitrance has provided them with an excuse for not investing in Russia. Consequently, the Japanese governing elite has seen China and other areas of Asia as more promising recipients of both aid and investment funds.

These perceptions have been both influenced and reinforced by the animosities generated on the political side. Many in the Japanese elite cannot see the issue of succoring democracy and moderation in Russia in the same terms as does the West, because Japan, unlike Western Europe and the United States, still has a specific national interest at stake which Russia has not satisfied. Many in Tokyo have therefore resented Western insistence that Japan give large-scale help to Russia, as tending to undermine Japanese negotiating leverage on Russia. The United States has become one of the objects of this resentment. Although Washington has never been the main source of the pressure on Japan—that being the West Europeans, and particularly Germany—it will be seen in the discussion below that during 1992 America nevertheless played an important role in helping to obtain (indeed, compel) Japanese acquiescence to the emerging plans for international assistance.

This U.S. behavior has been an unpleasant surprise to Tokyo. In the eyes of some Japanese, Washington's decision in 1992 to shift its weight toward support of major international funding for Russia was a step harmful to Japanese interests, and one that outweighed the importance of the verbal support the United States periodically paid to the justice of the Japanese claim to the Northern Territories.

On the other hand, despite its compulsory participation in international agreements to assist Russia, Japan has sought at every turn to minimize that participation to the degree politically feasible—that is, to do as little as it thinks consistent with not becoming isolated. Preoccupied with an unredeemed national interest not shared by the other major industrial states—the Northern Territories issue—Japan has acquired a reputation as the most reluctant and parsimonious of the leading industrial states in doling out assistance to Moscow. This perpetual foot-dragging is the more conspicuous because unlike the United States, whose help to Russia has also been fairly limited, Japan has a large pool of available capital that might have been drawn upon for this purpose. The Japanese posture toward Russia also contrasts with Japan's somewhat more benign attitude toward Mongolia and the Central Asian republics of the former Soviet Union, and even more with Tokyo's strong advocacy of international funding and investment for Vietnam.

For all these reasons, Japan has earned little political credit in Russia for what it has in fact done to help, and considerable blame for what it has not done. Although the Japanese Foreign Ministry has hoped that token amounts of "humanitarian assistance," mainly in the Russian Far East, would significantly soften local attitudes on the territorial issue, that has thus far not been the case.[32]

In sum, over the last two years the issue of assistance to Russia has come to embarrass Japan's relationships on all sides, creating new

---

[32]Here one must distinguish between attitudes of the relatively small population on the disputed islands themselves and attitudes of the much larger population of Sakhalin Oblast (which includes the islands) and the Russian Far East generally. There is some evidence to suggest that some of the inhabitants in the southern Kurils—perhaps as many as 50 percent—have become enticed by the prospective economic benefits of living under Japanese rule. (See the poll reported in *Rossiyskaya Gazeta*, July 30, 1992 [FBIS-SOV, August 12, 1992].) In Sakhalin Oblast as a whole and in the Far East more broadly, views seem much more adverse to giving up the islands.

sources of friction with Japan's friends in the West while worsening rather than improving the relationship with Russia.

EVOLUTION OF THE ISSUE OF ASSISTANCE

These dilemmas did not begin to emerge as a serious problem for Japan until fairly late in the Gorbachev era because of a widespread Western perception that the Soviet economy was still dominated by forces opposed to meaningful reform.[33]   Gorbachev declined to adopt the plan, worked out by the young Soviet economist Grigoriy Yavlinskiy and some American academics, for a "Grand Bargain" linking massive Western economic aid to radical Soviet reform. Like many in the West, Japanese officials considered the Yavlinskiy plan both overambitious and unrealistic; but Gorbachev's vague substitute plan, which held out little concrete promise of early reform, was completely disappointing.

Consequently, at the July 1990 Houston summit meeting of the "Group of Seven" leading Western industrial powers (the so-called G-7), despite some lobbying from Germany,[34] there was little support from most of the Western leaders for more than limited technical assistance to the Soviet Union because of general skepticism about Soviet willingness to move decisively toward market reform. The G-7 indefinitely deferred the issue of joint financial help to the USSR by requesting a detailed report on the question from the International Monetary Fund (IMF), the World Bank, and two other international agencies. (When that report eventually appeared the following spring, it was dubious about the value of financial aid to the USSR under existing circumstances.) In the meantime, Japan, which has

---

[33]In the immediate wake of the 1989 East European revolutions, Japan did come under some pressure from the United States to help the new East European democra- cies, and Premier Toshiki Kaifu in January 1990 felt obliged to respond by promising a package of nearly $2 billion in loans and credits to Poland and Hungary. This offer evoked considerable criticism at home for Kaifu from Japanese who believed it to have been unnecessary and extraneous to Japanese interests. But until much later the larger question of helping Gorbachev evoked no such problem.

[34]Before the summit, Chancellor Helmut Kohl sent a letter to all the summit partici- pants, including Japanese Premier Kaifu, urging large-scale international funding for Gorbachev. Kaifu's reply cited both continued Soviet military spending and the unre- solved Kurils territorial issue as reasons for rejecting this plea. (*Mainichi Shimbun*, August 7, 1990.)

always sought as much formal public support regarding the Northern Territories as it can get from its Western partners, had little difficulty obtaining from the G-7 leaders a paragraph in their final communiqué, noting the importance of settling the territorial dispute between Japan and the Soviet Union.

This situation began to alter in the late fall and winter of 1990, as many new complicating factors emerged in rapid succession. Because of the advance of the Soviet centrifugal process and Soviet economic disintegration, there was an accelerated decline in production and in export deliveries. By the end of the year Soviet hard currency reserves were rapidly falling, the internal distribution system was in considerable disarray, and there was widespread concern in the West over food shortages and the possibility of famine in Soviet cities. Against this background, in December 1990 Japan announced a decision to offer the Soviet Union a token credit of $100 million to be used only for "humanitarian purposes"—that is, for purchases of food and clothing in Japan, supposedly for prompt distribution in the Soviet Union during that winter. Although the credit would be "humanitarian" in nature, interest would be payable.

This gesture was evidently intended, among other things, to facilitate the upcoming April negotiations with Gorbachev. It did not do so, however, because rapid changes in the political and economic environment soon put the offer into the limbo where it long remained. As already noted, in the winter of 1990–1991 Gorbachev turned to the right to appease his reactionary domestic critics, and in January he authorized the use of force in the Baltic republics, with resultant bloodshed that caused widespread revulsion in the West. Almost simultaneously, the Soviet Union, its hard currency reserves dwindling, temporarily ceased paying its bills to foreign creditors, abruptly raising the issue of the viability of even "humanitarian" loans to Moscow.

During the three months leading up to Gorbachev's April visit to Japan, these twin developments on the political and economic fronts cast a shadow not only on the advisability of any Japanese economic assistance to Gorbachev, but also on the very future of the existing Soviet-Japanese trade relationship. Nevertheless, over precisely this period some leaders of the Liberal Democratic Party continued the long-drawn-out effort they had already begun, to coordinate in

Tokyo an economic package that might be presented to Gorbachev as the basis for a deal over the Northern Territories. This section of the Japanese governing elite was evidently encouraged to persevere because it noted that South Korea had in fact recently made a deal successfully trading large economic benefits to the Soviets for a mostly political recompense.[35] In March, as earlier recounted, LDP secretary-general Ozawa therefore carried to Moscow an unprecedented package of $26 billion in proposed loans in exchange for Soviet recognition of Japanese "residual sovereignty" over the four Northern Territories. Then, in April, Gorbachev paid his visit to Japan and rejected these Japanese terms for assistance to the Soviet economy.

This apparently was a turning point. In May, with the Gorbachev visit out of the way and the possibility of an early territorial deal discarded, Japanese banks completely suspended new loans to the USSR. By the end of May, the Soviet Union owed Japan some $515 million in unpaid bills, and the Ministry of International Trade and Investment halted the granting of government trade insurance for all large new Japanese contracts with the USSR.

Japanese worries now became focused on the run-up to the London summit of the G-7 nations scheduled for mid-July 1991. During the preliminary sparring, Germany[36] and France, supported by Italy,

---

[35]In January 1991, the Soviet Union and the Republic of Korea signed an agreement providing for the USSR to receive—despite the fact that it had just stopped paying its existing foreign debts—some $1 billion in new commercial bank loans and $2 billion in trade credits for the purchase of merchandise, plants, and equipment. The unstated political quid pro quo was the Soviet Union's continued movement away from support of the political objectives of North Korea, a process that had already brought about Moscow's September 1990 recognition of the Republic of Korea in defiance of the wishes of Kim Il-sung. The January 1991 economic agreement subsequently became controversial in Seoul because the bank loans to Moscow had to be raised in hard currency on the international market at a time when South Korea was itself running a current-account deficit. (*Far East Economic Review*, June 11, 1992.) The Japanese may have felt that given the Korean precedent, there was some chance that a similar but much larger offer could "purchase" the Northern Territories. The difference, of course, was that it was far easier politically for Gorbachev to abandon Kim Il-sung than to abandon the Northern Territories.

[36]As noted below, the German position as the most ardent international advocate of assistance to Moscow was to become steadily more pronounced through the summer of 1992. Since then, the German stance has become somewhat more tempered, as

emerged as the leading advocates of international financial assistance to Gorbachev, with Japan at the opposite pole as the leading opponent, and the United States in an intermediate position, but at this stage still leaning toward the Japanese side.[37] Early skirmishes were fought over the issue of whether Gorbachev was to be invited as a full participant to the G-7 summit (he eventually came as a "guest"), and whether the Soviet Union would be admitted to the IMF and thus be given access to IMF loans. (In the end, Gorbachev's regime was given essentially meaningless "associate" status, without eligibility for such loans.) Another symptom of the more charged atmosphere compared with the previous year's G-7 meeting was the fact that Japan was this time unable to get its territorial dispute with Moscow mentioned in the summit joint communiqué, because of the reluctance of some of the European states to imply that settlement of that dispute was a prerequisite for assistance to the USSR.

During the last two weeks preceding the summit, Gorbachev's adviser Yevgeniy Primakov visited Japan to lobby for a more forthcoming Japanese attitude at the G-7 meeting, after which Premier Kaifu visited the United States to lobby (among other things) for continued American rejection of these pleas. By the eve of the summit, some Japanese officials were for the first time seriously concerned about becoming "isolated."[38] However, in the end, the Japanese position at the summit was rescued by Gorbachev, who characteristically helped Western skeptics by once again vacillating on the question of Soviet economic reform.

As a result, despite the greater Western political pressure for financial help to the Soviet Union in 1991 as compared with 1990, the results were similar. To paper over their continued disagreement and inaction, the G-7 leaders at the conclusion of the summit resolved to send their finance ministers to Moscow to discuss future alternatives.

Germany's own economic difficulties have grown and as the Russian force presence on German soil (a key consideration in the German attitude) has continued to decline.

[37]In mid-June President Bush stated that the United States would find it hard to make a large cash contribution to any international effort to help Gorbachev. Both Japan and the United States protested in late June when the European Community decided to advance funds to the Soviet Union from the European Bank for Research and Development, to which Japan and the United States had given some resources in the expectation that assistance would be directed solely to Eastern Europe.

[38]*Washington Post,* June 25, 1991.

Within the next few weeks, however, the situation was radically transformed by the abortive August 1991 coup attempt and the consequent rise of Yeltsin to power.

In the immediate wake of the failed coup, the G-7 leaders jointly announced a decision to extend food and medicinal "humanitarian" aid promptly to the Soviet Union.[39] The Japanese leadership, for its part, was apparently cautiously encouraged by the initial signals furnished by the now-dominant Russian government, particularly during the visit of Khasbulatov and Kunadze to Japan in September. After the Khasbulatov visit, the Japanese consensus evidently decided that it was important for Japan to come forth at once with at least a token and conditional package of assistance, designed to whet the Soviet appetite for the more significant benefits that could follow a territorial deal, to hold out incentives for Soviet movement toward a market economy, and to demonstrate to Japan's Western partners a somewhat more forthcoming attitude on the assistance issue.[40]

Accordingly, in early October, in preparation for a trip by the Japanese Foreign Minister to Moscow and a simultaneous visit by the Japanese Finance Minister to a G-7 meeting in Bangkok, Tokyo announced a highly qualified $2.5 billion package intended—provided all the conditions were met—to revive Japanese trade and investment in the Soviet Union.[41] In mid-October, Foreign Minister Taro

---

[39]In response to this decision, Japan decided to provide an outright grant of 1 billion yen (some $7 million) worth of medicine and food to the Soviet Union, to be distributed through the Red Cross. After the collapse of the Soviet Union, this humanitarian assistance was eventually dispatched to Russia during the winter, largely in the Far East. (*Nihon Keizai Shimbun*, January 16, 1992.) Like the similar humanitarian help furnished by other Western states, this aid was surely needed and welcome, but was nonetheless minuscule and trivial in the context of fundamental Soviet economic problems.

[40]The European Community (EC) had just offered Moscow $1.5 billion in new credit guarantees for purchase of food and medicine, bringing the total EC food assistance to $2.4 billion. The United States had offered $2.5 billion in agricultural loan guarantees. These actions influenced Japan's sense of a need to be seen making a comparable gesture. (*Los Angeles Times*, October 9, 1991.)

[41]*Los Angeles Times*, October 9, 1991. This hypothetical package included some $500 million in low-interest credits from the Japanese Export-Import Bank for purchase in Japan of food, clothing, and transportation equipment; $200 million in more general credits from the Export-Import Bank to facilitate other Japanese exports to the USSR; and $1.8 billion in trade insurance for Japanese companies trading with the Soviet Union to cover the risk of Soviet default on repayment.

Nakayama came to Moscow for talks with both the declining Soviet government and the rising Russian government, and proposed establishment of a joint committee to consider the issues involved in implementing the new Japanese aid package. But Nakayama warned that nothing at all could be forthcoming until Japan obtained from the Soviet Union and also from its constituent republics—who now increasingly wielded the power of the purse in the USSR—guarantees for repayment of both the past debts and the new loans. This huge caveat was reiterated at the simultaneous October meeting of the G-7 finance ministers in Bangkok, where the industrial powers agreed that only "emergency humanitarian aid" could be furnished until four preconditions were accepted in the Soviet Union, one of which was acceptance of the collective liability of the union and its republics for repayment of the USSR's debts.[42]

But this condition was becoming more and more difficult to satisfy because the Soviet Union's centrifugal process was continuing to accelerate. As the fall and winter wore on, Soviet press opinion on both the right and left became more bitter about the illusory nature of the promised Japanese help. Soviet writers pointed out that the $1.8 billion in trade insurance for Japanese firms was not money that would be disbursed to the Soviet Union, but was a normal feature of past Japanese practice in trading with the USSR, which MITI had suspended in May. Further, they noted that the $500 million in promised humanitarian food and medicine aid was not a grant, but a loan that would have to be paid for with interest; moreover, it could be used only to buy commodities in Japan, at high prices; furthermore, it would become available only after the original $100 million promised in January 1991 was used up; and finally, even the use of that initial $100 million was still blocked by the stalemate over who would guarantee its repayment.[43]

Toward the end of 1991, there seemed for a time an increasing possibility that some Japanese assistance might actually soon arrive, but this prospect was then again deferred by the formal demise of the

---

[42]The other three preconditions were full disclosure of Soviet economic data, the creation of a comprehensive economic reform program, and the establishment of a responsible system for debt repayment.

[43]*Pravda*, October 11, 1991; *Komsomolskaya Pravda*, December 5, 1991; TASS, December 10, 1991.

Soviet Union in December. In late November, deputy foreign ministers of the G-7 powers, the Soviet Union, and eight of the twelve Soviet republics signed an agreement to defer for one year repayment of principal on Soviet foreign debts. Two weeks later, the Soviet press reported that the original $100 million in emergency food aid promised by Japan a year earlier might now finally be forthcoming as a result of a repayment guarantee offered by Ivan Silayev, the senior economic official in Gorbachev's Soviet regime. Ironically, however, within a few days any such guarantee was rendered moot by the formation of the Commonwealth of Independent States (CIS), putting an end to the Soviet state.

Now there was a replay of the events of the winter of 1990–1991, but on a larger scale. With the demise of the Soviet state, even token repayment of accumulated Soviet trade debts again halted completely, and the former Soviet Foreign Trade Bank, temporarily transferred to the CIS, was for the time being unable to maintain even interest payments on a large accumulation of trade credits guaranteed by foreign banks.[44] The Japanese government told Japanese banks to prepare for sizeable loan losses, MITI froze large sums previously earmarked as prospective cover for Soviet debts to Japanese companies, Japanese steel firms clamoured for their government to guarantee payment for pipe orders already committed to Russia, and an exasperated Premier Miyazawa remarked that political stability was a prerequisite for implementation of any economic assistance to the former Soviet Union.[45] Even the $100 million "humanitarian" credit for food and medicinal purchases, first promised a year earlier, was again put off as Japan awaited a reply from Moscow regarding who would now guarantee repayment and what state bank to deal with.[46]

---

[44]TASS, January 15, January 17, 1992. The Japanese press reported that a total of $800 million was by now at stake for Japanese banks. (TASS, January 17, 1992, citing *Yomiuri Shimbun*, January 17, 1992.)

[45]KYODO, December 10, 1991. The Japanese perception of developments in the former Soviet Union was vividly reflected in an early November interview with Deputy Vice Foreign Minister Koji Watanabe, who complained that the Russian criminal mafia was changing the destination of rail freight transportation leaving Vladivostok. *(Gaiko Forum*, Tokyo, December 1991.)

[46]Even greater difficulties were created for the very large long-term credits granted to Moscow by South Korea alluded to above. In December 1991, the Export-Import Bank of Korea for the time being closed its loan facility in Moscow amid great confusion as to which republics of the former Soviet Union would receive loans promised to

At this juncture, however, Japan once again began to come under pressure from the other Western states, this time to help the democratic and reformist forces survive in the successor states to the Soviet Union. The West now began more actively to consider early Russian admission to the IMF, while Japan at first remained cool to the notion. On the eve of a 50-nation meeting convened by the United States in January to consider emergency assistance to the CIS republics, the Japanese government for the first time decided to offer modest grant assistance to Russia, so as "to avoid international criticism that Japan only expresses its intention to provide loans, but is reluctant to provide grant-type aid."[47]   After some internal contention, Tokyo allocated a grant of $50 million for this purpose for Foreign Minister Watanabe to announce at the January conference as Japan's contribution to the drive for international humanitarian assistance. This gift was in addition to the much larger conditional loans and credits previously announced but not yet provided.[48]

By now, in early 1992, no less than four echelons of prospective Japanese economic assistance to Russia could be visualized as stacked up in ascending order, all awaiting satisfaction of various preconditions for fulfillment. Closest to realization was the new $50 million emergency food and medicine grant, although even delivery of that small tranche of Japanese help was temporarily slowed by administrative dislocations in Russia. Meanwhile, most of the $100 million humanitarian loan announced in January 1991 and the $2.5 billion package announced in October 1991 remained suspended because of the internal disarray in the former Soviet Union and the continued failure to arrive at an understanding as to who would guarantee repayment. Still further over the horizon, presumably awaiting a territorial settlement acceptable to Japan, was the question of whether Japan would ever revive the much larger $26 billion

Gorbachev and which would guarantee repayment. By now about half of $3 billion in credits offered to Gorbachev had already been disbursed.

[47] *Nihon Keizai Shimbun*, January 16, 1992.

[48] The Japanese press reported that the Foreign Ministry had wished to extend $100 million, but the Finance Ministry had insisted on less, and won the argument. The $50 million grant Japan now offered was in addition to the small $7 million grant already mentioned. (*Nihon Keizai Shimbun*, January 16, 1992.) The food and other commodities purchased with the grant were intended to be entirely distributed in the Russian Far East, including Sakhalin. (KYODO, January 16, 1992.)

package that Ozawa had privately presented to Gorbachev in March 1991 but which Japan had never publicly acknowledged.

MITI remained reluctant to insure large-scale Japanese investments in Russia, and without such insurance, Japanese companies remained reluctant to take meaningful new investment initiatives.[49] The broad political and economic impasse between Russia and Japan continued. In late December, when Japan formally acknowledged Russia to be the successor state to the Soviet Union, Foreign Minister Kozyrev had taken the political risk of explicitly reaffirming the legality and validity of the 1956 Joint Declaration, including the clause about the handover of Shikotan and the Habomais.[50] The Russian Far Eastern lobby reacted, as before, with threats to secede from Russia if even these two islands were surrendered, while Japan reacted, also as before, with a cool reiteration of its position that it could not accept a two-island solution.[51]

The prolonged double impasse, in turn, had a visible impact on the mutual perceptions and, indeed, emotions, of both Russian and Japanese leaders. In late January, Yeltsin met Miyazawa at the United Nations in New York and said that the Yeltsin visit to Japan that the two sides had begun planning could not take place until September, far later than Tokyo had expected. Thus Japan would be the last industrialized democracy to be visited by Yeltsin.[52] The following week, when Foreign Minister Watanabe visited Moscow for talks with Kozyrev, Japan was seriously embarrassed when a scheduled Watanabe meeting with Yeltsin was abruptly cancelled with lit-

---

[49]The leading potential exception at this point was the large project of a Japanese-American consortium to explore reserves of oil and gas off Sakhalin. In early 1992, MITI officials were reported to be prepared to grant credits and insurance to allow work to begin on this project because it had been under discussion with Moscow for two decades—and also, presumably, because the prospective economic benefits for Japan were considerable. *(New York Times,* February 7, 1992.) However, by late 1992 no Japanese government money had in fact been furnished for this purpose, largely because approval of the project had been delayed by internal disputes in Russia.

[50]On December 27, the news agency INTERFAX reported that Kozyrev had stated this in a meeting with the Japanese ambassador, and two days later Kozyrev said much the same in a television interview. (Moscow television, December 29, 1992 [FBIS-SOV, December 31, 1991].)

[51]*International Herald Tribune,* December 31, 1991.

[52]*International Herald Tribune,* December 31, 1991.

tle attempt at explanation. This behavior reinforced all the old prej-
udices about Russia entrenched in the Japanese Foreign Ministry.
One unidentified Japanese diplomat commented at this time:

> The whole world is looking at Russia as a splendid new country that
> should be praised. Of course, they have abandoned Communism.
> But for us, it is basically the same country. The people are the same.
> And I think we have a difficult neighbor again.[53]

THE UNITED STATES SPLITS FROM JAPAN ON AID TO YELTSIN

Ironically, it was against this background of cooling Japanese relations with Yeltsin that pressure began to build in Washington during
the early spring of 1992 for the United States to take a more active
role in leading the West to help Russia. The latest in a series of international agreements to reschedule some of the former Soviet
Union's debts was to expire at the end of March unless renewed.
Yeltsin was meanwhile facing a meeting of the Russian Congress of
People's Deputies on April 6 that was expected to present a fundamental challenge to the entire course of reform. In several letters
and phone calls to President Bush, Yeltsin is said to have stressed the
need for Western help to defeat this challenge, and Foreign Minister
Kozyrev reiterated the appeal in a Brussels meeting with Secretary of
State Baker on March 10.[54] Simultaneously, the strong case for more
decisive American action was being vigorously argued in a debate
begun by former President Nixon within the U.S. elite.

On March 27, deputy finance ministers of the G-7 countries, including Japan, met in Paris to urgently consider Russian financial needs
for the remainder of the year. They now agreed to establish a $6 bil-
lion fund to stabilize the ruble, to be financed through the IMF. They
also discussed a mutual commitment to provide to Moscow an additional sum three times that amount—partly through the IMF, but
mostly on a bilateral basis—to fill the anticipated gap in Russia's balance of payments in 1992. However, this issue of balance-of-pay-

---

[53] *International Herald Tribune,* December 31, 1991.

[54] *Washington Post,* April 9, 1992.

ments help was contentious within the G-7, and public recriminations subsequently emerged among the participating countries about
exactly what understandings were reached.[55]

These opposing versions of what had been agreed surfaced publicly
after President Bush and Chancellor Kohl in separate announce-
ments on April 1 proclaimed a joint commitment by the G-7 group to
provide Russia with the full package of $24 billion for ruble stabiliza-
tion plus balance-of-payments support.[56] Soon thereafter, Tokyo
reacted with unusual candor in expressing its anger and dismay,
denying that it had agreed to this figure, and asserting that it was
"inappropriate and premature" for the President to have announced
the package before working out the details with Japan.[57]

Japan saw this package as threatening to undercut its leverage on
Russia on the territorial issue in three ways. First, it presaged immi-
nent Russian admission to the IMF (in fact, consummated in late
April) and access to IMF and World Bank credits, funded in part by
Japan's ongoing commitments to these international organizations.[58] Moreover, the package announced by America and Germany
would automatically include new, additional Japanese money that

---

[55]A senior Japanese official later said that the meeting had discussed providing $12
billion in balance-of-payments relief, with an additional $6 billion as a possibility if the
$12 billion proved insufficient. (New York Times, April 5, 1992.) But Russian Vice
Premier Gaidar—preparing for the admission of his country to the IMF—had given the
IMF an estimate that a full $18 billion would be required for this purpose. Afterward,
Japanese officials contended that although this sum was discussed at the Paris G-7
meeting, it was not formally approved.   American officials, on the other hand, responded that the entire target sum of about $18 billion had been "discussed and gen-
erally approved" by the participants, while German official sources characteristically
went further, describing the Japanese account of the proceedings as "completely in-
explicable." (Washington Post, April 9, 1992.)

[56]New York Times, April 2, 1992. Japan received no warning before Germany made its
announcement, and only a few hours warning before the United States did so.

[57]New York Times, April 4, 1992.

[58]Thus the $18 billion balance-of-payments help promised Russia included some $4.5
billion in IMF and World Bank loans. Some Japanese contended that the $4.5 billion
figure was an underestimate, and that Russia would become entitled to greater IMF
funds after the total capital available to the IMF rose as planned in the fall of 1992.
(Nihon Keizai Shimbun, April 6, 1992.) Moreover, Japan feared that the 1992 funding
for Russia was only the beginning, and that it would be pinned down to furnishing
large funds to Russia through international channels year after year without resolution
of the territorial issue.

would have to be supplied to the IMF as Japan's share of the new $6 billion ruble stabilization fund when it eventually materialized.[59] A mere six weeks earlier, Deputy Foreign Minister Kunihiko Saito, in Moscow for working-level negotiations on the territorial dispute, had publicly remarked that only after Japan had obtained a promise of the islands' return or at least "a clear indication that this problem will be solved in a certain clearly limited period of time" would Japan "be in a position to go along with other G-7 countries in various projects to help Russia, *such as the establishment of a stabilization fund.*"[60] (Emphasis added.) By the end of March, the United States, by siding with Germany, had forced Japan to abandon this attempt to hold the stabilization fund hostage to the territorial dispute.

Second, the G-7 decision seemed at the time to preempt and override early Japanese misgivings about rescheduling certain of the foreign debts Russia had inherited from the Soviet Union. (In practice, the rescheduling issue was not immediately settled, and remained a matter of protracted dispute in the West.)[61]

---

[59]Immediately after the announcement of the package, a senior Japanese Foreign Ministry official lamented that it would be unavoidable for Japan to furnish its normal quota of IMF dues to this new fund, which would be set up under a special IMF mechanism called the "General Agreements to Borrow." Since Japan's share of contributions to IMF capital was normally 12.5 percent, it expected to owe about $750 million in new money for the $6 billion fund for ruble stabilization. (KYODO, April 2, 1992.)

[60]*International Herald Tribune*, February 12, 1992. Saito at the time had some reason to assume that this Japanese attitude toward the stabilization fund was consistent with the international consensus. In late January, officials of the leading industrialized nations meeting in Garden City, New York, had rejected as premature a British proposal for creation of a ruble stabilization fund. *(The Wall Street Journal*, April 28, 1992.)

[61]In the spring of 1992, it was anticipated that as soon as the IMF credit installments began flowing to Russia, this would trigger a more general process of renegotiating the debts of the former Soviet Union through the Paris Club, an organization of private lending organizations of Western creditor nations that generally waits for IMF blessing of an economic reform program and the start of IMF financing. *(The Wall Street Journal*, June 26, 1992.) Nevertheless, a running dispute continued throughout 1992 on the issue of rescheduling old Soviet debt, with some Western creditors insisting on only short-term renewals of debt moratoria, while others (chiefly the United States) prepared to accept the much longer postponement requested by the Russians. Until December 1992, the Germans, with much greater Soviet and Russian debt exposure, maintained a more demanding attitude than Japan on the debt moratorium issue, but by the close of the year Chancellor Kohl had begun to give ground to Yeltsin's demand for a long-term moratorium on repayment of the old Soviet debts.

And third, the G-7 package as announced by Bush and Kohl purported to include large new sums, as yet unidentified, of additional bilateral cash outlays to Russia,[62] presumably from those countries that could best afford it. Japan bridled at the hint that it was one such country, and soon made it clear that unless there were a territorial settlement with Russia, it could not provide any new bilateral money beyond $100 million pledged in January 1991 and the $2.5 billion package announced in October 1991, *all* of which was yet to be implemented.

As it turned out, most of the multilateral portion of the G-7 package was not in fact delivered to Moscow during 1992 because of Russian economic and political disarray. But in the spring of 1992, this was not what Japan expected to happen, and Japanese leaders therefore began to draw a firmer distinction between Japanese assistance to Russia flowing through international organizations and direct bilateral Japanese aid to Russia.[63] Indeed, some Japanese officials suggested to the Japanese press that Tokyo would compensate for the funds it was being forced to supply Russia through international channels by reducing the amount it would provide to Russia directly.[64] It will be seen later that this consideration may have affected Japanese behavior toward Yeltsin during the negotiations prior to his aborted September 1992 visit to Japan.

Japanese Foreign Ministry officials in the spring of 1992 gave unattributed interviews in the Tokyo press agonizing over the conse-

---

[62]There was a good deal of initial confusion as to how much of the $24 billion package was new. U.S. officials asserted that although some of this money represented earlier bilateral commitments to Russia, new money would be provided by the $6 billion stabilization fund, by $4.5 billion promised in multilateral IMF credits for balance-of-payments support, and some $3 to $4 billion in additional (but as yet unidentified) bilateral commitments from individual nations. *(The Wall Street Journal,* April 8, 1992.)

[63]*New York Times,* April 4, 1992. At the end of April, Foreign Minister Watanabe in an interview with a Russian newspaper professed willingness to render aid to Russian reforms despite the Kurils dispute. He made it clear, however, that he meant the help through international channels arranged by the G-7 and the bilateral "humanitarian" help Japan had already offered, but not any other significant bilateral assistance. *(Komsomolskaya Pravda,* April 27, 1992.)

[64]*Nihon Keizai Shimbun,* April 6, 1992. In fact, little or no such direct assistance from Japan had yet materialized.

quences the new international decisions would have for their territorial negotiations with Moscow. There had been "a U.S. policy
change," they said, which "will have a subtle impact on Russia's attitude in its negotiations with Japan," and there were "misgivings that
Japan's principle of inseparability between politics and economics
will in effect be rendered null and void." Until recently, the Foreign
Ministry officials observed, Japanese policy toward Russia had been
fortified by "the U.S. pledge to take a discreet attitude toward
Russia." But now, "with the change in U.S. policy, and with
Germany—which is at the forefront of positive aid to Russia—playing
the role of chairman" [at the upcoming Munich summit of the G-7 in
July], "there is a feeling of impending crisis within the government
that Japan will be put in a painful situation" in Munich. The Foreign
Ministry thought that "as a result of the U.S. displaying a positive
posture of extending aid to Russia. . .we will be in trouble if Russia
comes to think that nothing needs to be done about the territorial issue at a time when she was on the very point of having to do something about it." In short, the Japanese government feared that the
recent international decisions regarding aid to Russia would have "a
very negative effect on the negotiations being conducted between
Japan and Russia."[65] Some Japanese went so far as to term the
American change in position on this issue to have been a surprise
inflicted on Japan comparable in importance to the "Nixon shock"
twenty years earlier when Washington shifted from hostility to rapprochement with Beijing without warning to Japan.[66]

THE KURILS ISSUE AND THE MUNICH G-7 MEETING

After these watershed events, the Japanese government sought to
shore up its ability to defend its interests on the territorial issue at the
July G-7 summit meeting in Munich. In late April and early May,
Prime Minister Miyazawa visited Germany and France—the two
powers that were in the forefront of the drive to help Russia whether
or not the Kurils issue was ever resolved—with the avowed aim of
appealing for support on the territorial issue. Although Japanese political leaders assured the Japanese public of their satisfaction with

---

[65]*Nihon Keizai Shimbun,* April 4, 1992.

[66]*Nihon Keizai Shimbun,* July 13, 1992.

the tepid expressions of sympathy they received, the real results of Miyazawa's appeals were hardly encouraging, although predictable. Within a week after the Miyazawa visit, Chancellor Kohl made his strongest and most direct public criticism of Japan to date, saying that Germany had done as much as it could to finance economic and political change in the countries of the former Soviet Union and Eastern Europe, and that the time had come for Japan to "contribute more than it has up to now toward this reform effort." Kohl warned Tokyo that "to play a waiting game and save in the wrong place would be the worst of all possible investments in our common future."[67] This was perhaps the high-water mark of aggressive German advocacy of Western assistance to Russia.

Simultaneously, Foreign Minister Watanabe visited Kazakhstan and Kyrgyzstan, two of the former Soviet republics of Central Asia, appealing to them to use their influence with the Russians to facilitate a territorial settlement on Japanese terms, and hinting at Japanese economic rewards that might be forthcoming for those who did so. This effort had very little hope of success from the start. The newly independent Central Asian states were unlikely in any case to have great influence on Russian behavior on the Kurils issue. Moreover, although eager to obtain whatever economic largesse might be forthcoming from Japan, they were by no means ready to jeopardize their delicate and still extremely important ongoing relations with Russia. They therefore responded with sympathetic but vigorously noncommital noises to the Japanese pleas.[68]

---

[67]*New York Times*, May 6, 1992, which also quoted an international banking institute as estimating that between September 1990 and February 1992, Germany had offered the republics of the former Soviet Union some $45 billion in total commitments, Italy some $6.2 billion, and the United States some $5 billion. Japan had proposed only $2.6 billion, all still unrealized.

[68]Kyrgyz President Akayev expressed sympathy for Japan but observed that "Russia is a major power" and "it is necessary to take heed not to intervene in Russia's internal affairs." Kazakh President Nazarbayev emphasized that the territorial issue was a bilateral one and "we do not intend to expand the area of involvement." *Asahi Shimbun* (May 4, 1992), in reporting this, noted rather derisively that the Watanabe trip to Central Asia had been planned in the Foreign Ministry to coincide with the Miyazawa trip to France and Germany in order (in the words of one ministry official) to "press Russia for a decision by forming an international encircling net." Obviously, the ministry miscalculated the relative forces at work.

Tokyo's biggest efforts to elicit support, however, were as usual directed at the United States. In mid-June, on the eve of Yeltsin's visit to Washington, Miyazawa noted publicly that President Bush had assured him that the territorial dispute would be raised in the President's talks with Yeltsin. Moreover, Miyazawa made it clear that he expected this intervention to bear some fruit for the Munich G-7 meeting in July. "I don't want this to be handled as our problem alone," he said, "but as a common problem of the Group of Seven."[69]

This Japanese campaign to "internationalize" the territorial dispute was an unusually overt effort to induce the major Western powers to join at last in placing pressure on Russia to accommodate Japan.[70] In effect, Tokyo was seeking to get its partners to make a Northern Territories settlement an implied condition for continuing the international economic rescue effort. But that effort had been launched because of an overriding Western perception of a common vested interest in Yeltsin's survival. When visualized in these terms, there could be little hope of Japanese success. The Japanese campaign did, however, dramatize for the other members of the G-7 the political importance Japan attached to the Northern Territories issue. It thus forewarned Japan's partners that there was no prospect of obtaining significant *voluntary* Japanese cooperation with the rescue effort for Russia—beyond the funds Japan was obliged to furnish through international channels—until the territorial question was resolved.

Meanwhile, the Japanese attempt to "internationalize" the territorial dispute evoked considerable fresh acrimony with Russia in the early summer of 1992. There was a deterioration in the tone of the debate between Moscow and Tokyo as the Munich meeting grew closer. In late May, Yeltsin had reiterated his willingness to try to accelerate the five stages necessary to solve the territorial problem. Although he warned that "final resolution" of the territorial issue would be "impossible in either 1993 or 1994," he still expressed hope that a

---

[69]KYODO, June 17, 1992.

[70]Japan wanted more than lip service from the West. In late June, Deputy Foreign Minister Koichiro Matsuura stated that because of Japanese insistence, it was now "certain" that this time the Northern Territories issue would be mentioned in the G-7 summit documents, but that this was not the main point. "What is important," he said, "is how the issue will be discussed at the summit." (Interview in *Sankei Shimbun*, June 30, 1992.)

peace treaty could be signed in 1993.[71] A month later, however, after returning from his highly successful trip to the United States, Yeltsin's attitude toward Japan became more assertive. He reiterated that Russian-Japanese economic cooperation "cannot be made to depend on a political solution of the territorial dispute." He dramatically attacked Japan as "the only country that has not yet invested anything in Russia—not a cent, not half a dollar, not half a yen." He added that "maybe we will talk with Japan about the islands" after "good relations and good cooperation have been established."[72] By this time, Yeltsin was reported determined to avoid any private meeting alone with Miyazawa at the Munich G-7 summit, and at the last moment he ordered postponement of a scheduled session of the Russo-Japanese group working on a draft peace treaty until after the summit.[73]

As the Munich summit approached, the Moscow press became indignant about the "naked politics" practiced by Japan in attempting to "gain support from the major European capitals in exerting pressure on Moscow" over the territorial issue.[74] In early July, Yeltsin's close adviser Genadiy Burbulis, who chaired the Russian commission preparing the Yeltsin September visit to Japan, denounced Japan's attempts to internationalize the dispute and insisted that Russia would not tolerate any pressure to solve the territorial issue "at any price."[75]

Most telling of all was the Russian perception of the U.S. factor in the wake of Yeltsin's visit to Washington. Alluding to Japan's appeals to the United States, one Russian Foreign Ministry expert observed that American support for the Japanese stand on the territorial dispute had had "no effect on Russian-American ties whatsoever."[76] This was evidently indeed the case, despite the American government's verbal support for the Japanese territorial claims. Neither those in the U.S. elite who strongly advocated major economic help for

---

[71]Interview in *Komsomolskaya Pravda*, May 27, 1992.

[72]*Komsomolskaya Pravda*, July 3, 1992.

[73]ITAR-TASS, June 24, June 27, July 3, 1992.

[74]*Rossiyskaya Gazeta*, June 22, 1992.

[75]INTERFAX, July 4, 1992.

[76]INTERFAX, July 6, 1992.

Yeltsin nor those who opposed such help as useless or beyond American means were perceptibly influenced in either direction by the Japanese grievance against Russia.

In the end, the Munich G-7 summit of July 1992 gave Japan only a minimum of face-saving satisfaction on the territorial issue. The final summit "political declaration" called in neutral fashion for "full normalization of Japan-Russia relations by resolving the territorial issue," but did not support the Japanese position or even mention the Northern Territories directly.[77] Yeltsin, before leaving Moscow for Munich, professed Russia's willingness to reach a fair solution to the dispute, but insisted that the G-7 summit was not the forum to resolve it. The next day, he volunteered that Russia might be more willing to settle the issue if Japan were more willing to provide assistance. He was strikingly more forthcoming on other political issues that seemed of greater concern to the West—and that were of less direct concern to Japan—volunteering reassurances that Russian troops would leave the Baltics and that Russia and Ukraine were achieving a rapprochement.[78]

Meanwhile, the G-7 summit in effect ratified the international economic decisions about Russia adopted in the spring, and cut some corners to begin to put them into effect. To help Yeltsin withstand the internal pressures he was under to emasculate economic reform and reject the IMF's painful prerequisites for international assis-

---

[77] *Washington Post*, July 8, 1992. The French and Germans were strongly opposed even to mentioning the territorial issue, but were forced to yield, presumably because of U.S. support for Japan. France, however, is said to have been particularly insistent that the statement abstain from supporting the Japanese side of the territorial controversy. Despite Tokyo's defeat on that point, Japanese leaders portrayed the weak summit statement at home—particularly during the subsequent election campaign—as an "unprecedented success for Japanese diplomacy." (*Yomiuri Shimbun*, July 10, 1992, cited by *Izvestiya*, July 10, 1992.)

[78] *The Wall Street Journal*, July 9, 1992. The West had given Yeltsin—and Japan—strong indication as to which of these political issues it considered most important. According to a "senior French official," the G-7 had decided before the summit to ask Yeltsin, as a sign of good faith, not to send fresh reinforcements to the Baltics and to begin immediate reductions in troop levels there. Yeltsin preempted the request by volunteering a pledge on the subject. (*Washington Post*, July 8, 1992.) To be sure, the durability of even this pledge eventually proved shaky, since Yeltsin a few months later was compelled by Russian nationalist pressures to announce a temporary halt to the withdrawal from the Baltic states.

tance,[79] several Western countries, led by the United States, had urged the IMF to relax its demands on Yeltsin sufficiently to start the conduit of financial help flowing soon to Moscow. As a result, by the eve of the summit the IMF had moved to scale down—in effect, to stretch out—its demands in negotiations with the Russian government, while simultaneously agreeing to grant Moscow immediately an initial tranche of $1 billion in IMF loans prior to satisfaction of any of those demands. A $600 million credit from the World Bank would accompany this initial IMF installment. More IMF balance-of-payments credits would supposedly be forthcoming only if Russia by the autumn of 1992 demonstrated sufficient progress in reducing its budget deficit and bringing down inflation. And the $6 billion ruble stabilization fund would supposedly come into being only in 1993, and only if Russian inflation were brought down to levels common in the West, and if the budget were approaching balance. The G-7 summit, approving this decision, also endorsed a "serious" rescheduling of official debt by the governmental and commercial banks belonging to the Paris Club. Meanwhile, it was anticipated that some G-7 nations would now unfreeze lines of official export credit that had been held in suspension.[80]

The Japanese reaction to all this activity was to conclude that "Yeltsin's threat from the weak had dominated the summit from first to last,"[81] and that Tokyo "had been forced to make a concession"

---

[79]Before Yeltsin reached agreement with the IMF, he publicly attacked the organization for attempting to impose requirements on Russia that were too rigid, and claimed he was willing if necessary to forgo the promised billions from the IMF. These statements were generally regarded as intended to disarm his domestic critics and to induce Western capitals to come to his aid in his negotiations with the IMF. (*New York Times, Washington Post,* July 5, 1992; *The Wall Street Journal,* July 6, 1992.)

[80]With the unfreezing of these credits, some of the $11 billion in bilateral aid to Russia promised as part of the $24 billion package would now also begin to flow. (Philip Hanson in *Post–Soviet/East European Report,* RFE/RL Research Institute, Vol. 9, No. 30, July 20, 1992.) By early July, Japan also had resumed long-stalled talks with Russia about reinstating trade insurance for investments in the energy field. MITI had been studying resumption of such trade insurance ever since Tokyo suspended it in 1991, but the negotiations had been suspended because of uncertainty over repayment guarantees. (*Nihon Keizai Shimbun,* July 1, 1992.) Soon after the summit, the Bank of Tokyo was authorized to provide $360 million in loans to the Russian Bank of Foreign Economic Affairs to help Russia pay unpaid bills to nine Japanese trading companies. (KYODO, July 17, 1992.)

[81]*Nihon Keizai Shimbun,* July 13, 1992.

because the G-7 was unwilling to allow Yeltsin to return home empty-handed. One Foreign Ministry official grumbled that the IMF had up to then provided loans to its member nations only when their reform efforts were recognized, "and international financial organizations should stick to their rules." Some Japanese now feared that there might be further slippage in the IMF requirements imposed on Russia if Moscow in the future were unable to meet them—as seemed all too likely—and that eventually the rest of the $24 billion package would follow the initial $1 billion installment whether or not the Russian budget and inflation were brought under control.[82]

Meanwhile, the Japanese government could at least congratulate itself that it had fought off two suggestions regarding Russia posed at the G-7 summit which it found particularly obnoxious. One was the idea that Russia might be invited to join the G-7 club of major industrial states, a notion voiced in an offhand manner by President Bush shortly before the summit. Mr. Bush evidently mentioned this possibility only as a gesture to Yeltsin, did not personally endorse the proposal, and did not expect it to bear fruit.[83] However, the Japanese government was indignant and "disgusted" that the idea had even been put forward for discussion at the summit,[84] and a number of Japanese politicians, including former LDP secretary-general Ozawa, went out of their way to denounce the suggestion.[85] In the end, the idea received virtually no support at the summit, and was soon dismissed.

A more serious skirmish won by the Japanese at the summit concerned a German-French proposal for a new $700 million multilateral fund to administer a program to improve the safety of Soviet-

---

[82]*Yomiuri Shimbun,* July 1, 1992. In fact, however, by the close of 1992 this had not happened. Although much of the bilateral portion of the IMF credit package promised to Russia was indeed provided by Western countries before the end of the year, some was not. Meanwhile, after the initial installment, the bulk of the multilateral portion of the package was not released by the IMF in 1992 because of delays in Russian satisfaction of IMF criteria. This fact has generated repeated complaints in Russia that the West was failing to live up to its promises to help.

[83]Mr. Bush characteristically said he "expected summit participants to discuss the possibility of Russia joining the G-7, but he wasn't endorsing the idea." (*The Wall Street Journal,* July 3, 1992.)

[84]*Nihon Keizai Shimbun,* July 4, 1992.

[85]*Nihon Keizai Shimbun,* July 5, 1992.

designed nuclear reactors. While professing readiness in principle to help toward this aim, Tokyo was opposed to creating yet another international vehicle for draining money from Japan to Russia, and this time the United States supported Japan.[86] Much to German chagrin, the G-7 left most future aid for former Soviet nuclear reactors to be decided through bilateral agreements between the former Soviet republics and G-7 members. Thus Japan could continue to calibrate how much it did in this realm to suit its political requirements.[87]

THE ROAD TO CANCELLATION OF THE YELTSIN VISIT

During the two months between the Munich G-7 summit and the Russian president's scheduled September 1992 visit to Japan, trends in both Moscow and Tokyo made the possibility of an accommodation even more doubtful.

In Russia, because of the economic hardship that had accompanied the government's faltering efforts to move toward a market system, Yeltsin's political support, although still considerable, had been gradually sinking. Ironically, the same internal pressures that made Russia badly need Japanese help also made it increasingly difficult for Yeltsin to offer sufficient concessions to Japan to get that help. Many who had been allied with him in Gorbachev's time were now opposing him, and he now had reliable backing from only a minority in the legislature. A number of figures associated with reactionary institutions of the old Soviet regime—some closely associated with the coup leaders—had begun to reappear in positions of prominence, including some appointed by the leadership of the legislature.[88] An associated effort had begun to try to rehabilitate and

---

[86]Washington was said to have been particularly unhappy with the European proposal that the fund should be administered by the London-based European Bank for Reconstruction and Development, which was less susceptible to U.S. influence than the IMF or the World Bank. (*The Wall Street Journal,* July 9, 1992.)

[87]In January, Japan and the new U.S. administration did agree to a multilateral fund, but their contributions remained in question. (*New York Times,* January 29, 1993.)

[88]Thus in August 1992 Khasbulatov was reported to have appointed Col. Gen. Vladislav Achalov to an important job as a personal aide. Achalov was formerly head of Soviet airborne forces and participated in the 1991 Soviet military crackdown in the Baltics. He had supported the August 1991 attempted coup. Khasbulatov was also re-

justify the imprisoned coup leaders. Certain leaders of parliament, particularly Khasbulatov, were forming alliances with conservative forces in a concerted effort to trim Yeltsin's personal authority and force drastic policy changes on him. Many were now denouncing the Yeltsin leadership for relying too much on Western help, and for following a disastrous domestic policy to please the West. Some were going beyond that, to condemn the Yeltsin foreign policy as being too Western-oriented generally, and not sufficiently prepared to defend Russia's own national interests, particularly to the south and east of Russia. Some of Yeltsin's advisers, such as the opportunistic former democrat Sergey Stankevich, were also pressing for a rejection of reliance on the West and the IMF and for a turn toward a more authoritarian and nationalist policy. There was growing pressure on Yeltsin to abandon Premier Gaidar, symbol of the internal reform process, as well as Foreign Minister Kozyrev, symbol of the pro-Western foreign policy.

More specifically, Yeltsin had come under intensified pressure from a bloc of leaders of Russian heavy industry to drastically slow down the marketization process and to avoid complying with the demands levied on Russia by the IMF as preconditions for future IMF loans to stabilize the ruble and pay for Russian imports. These industrial managers were particularly anxious over the prospect that Moscow might cut off the huge subsidies flowing to their money-losing factories in order to comply with IMF insistence on balancing the budget and slowing inflation. The "industrialists" held a potent political weapon over Yeltsin—and the IMF—with the threat of mass unemployment if the subsidies were halted and the factories closed. Yeltsin therefore walked a tightrope in dealing with these people, who in conjunction with other Yeltsin opponents had built a broad political alliance with substantial popular support. While still trying to keep his ties with the West and the IMF, Yeltsin during 1992 made repeated concessions to the forces opposed to the course requested by the IMF. One notable such concession was his appointment of a head of the State Bank, Viktor Gerashchenko, who had little sympathy with marketization and who was determined to maintain subsidies to heavy industry regardless of the inflationary consequences.

---

ported to have made former KGB first deputy chief Filip Bobkov his personal security adviser. (RFE/RL Daily Report, August 14, 1992, on Sovset computer network.)

The net result was that Russian economic policy had become increasingly hesitant and self-contradictory, so that it became problematical whether the IMF's minimum criteria could be satisfied and whether all of the international financial help which the G-7 planned to extend to Russia—including $2.6 billion coerced from the Japanese—would in fact be delivered.[89]

Simultaneously, Yeltsin's control over his military had also become uncertain, and there seemed some disturbing parallels with Gorbachev's relations with the military in the winter of 1990–1991. To be sure, throughout 1992 Yeltsin's position relative to the generals was never quite as weak as Gorbachev's had been. When he was willing to spend his political capital, he seemed, for example, to retain some capacity to override military objections on arms control matters. Thus Yeltsin disregarded the wishes of many senior officers by agreeing to extraordinary concessions to the United States during the summer of 1992, first in acceding to a far-reaching nuclear agreement in Washington, and then in forcing an openly recalcitrant General Staff to yield to an American demand that it provide evidence to prove Moscow's claim that it had ceased violating the 1972 biological weapons treaty. Yet even on these matters, the deterioration in his overall domestic position sometimes obliged him to equivocate, for a time placing in doubt the nuclear commitments he agreed to in Washington.

Meanwhile, Yeltsin was always far more cautious in dealing with the assertive line publicly adopted by many generals on nationality and territorial issues—obviously because here the military seemed to find powerful backing from the extreme nationalist tendencies growing in the civilian elite. In this realm, several senior officers became openly insubordinate, contradicting Yeltsin publicly without apparent fear of punishment. For example, on one occasion a public Yeltsin pledge to withdraw Russian forces from Moldova was publicly contradicted by military leaders. Subsequently, after Yeltsin appointed Lt. Gen. Aleksandr Lebed to command Russian forces in Moldova,

---

[89]The figure of $2.6 billion, cited by a former Japanese official in October 1992, is the Japanese share of the $24 billion in bilateral and multilateral assistance agreed upon in principle by the G-7 in the spring and summer of 1992. By the end of the year, however, most of this Japanese share had not in fact been disbursed to Russia, largely because most of the multilateral portion of the G-7 package had not been delivered.

Lebed immediately took the occasion to give newspaper interviews savagely mocking Yeltsin's journey to Munich to seek help from the G-7 summit. Lebed was not punished. Other senior officers have on occasion expressed similar disagreement with Yeltsin, although not as flamboyantly.

One such case that had a direct impact on the dispute with Japan was a statement by Defense Minister Grachev contradicting a Yeltsin pledge to accelerate the total demilitarization of the Northern Territories as a good-will gesture to Japan. Although the Japanese Foreign Ministry asked Moscow to explain the Grachev statement, no credible answer was forthcoming. Yeltsin had appointed Grachev as Minister of Defense in the spring in an evident effort to pacify the military, despite much previous speculation that he would appoint a civilian.

These Yeltsin problems with the military, when combined with his broader political difficulties, played a major role in the internal Russian struggle over Yeltsin's forthcoming trip to Japan. In the summer of 1992, the Supreme Soviet held extended hearings and debates on the Japanese question, and Yeltsin's opponents sought with some success to use the hearings to constrain Yeltsin's negotiating flexibility. Presenting the Supreme Soviet with a long document prepared by the General Staff, Russia's military leaders now made a frontal appeal to his adversaries in parliament to cancel the troop cuts he had promised in the Kurils and to avoid any territorial concessions to Japan.[90] Although the General Staff said it accepted the validity of Khrushchev's 1956 Joint Declaration with Japan (which had offered to relinquish two of the islands), the military presentation nevertheless seemed to oppose even a two-island solution, despite the fact that Foreign Minister Kozyrev had endorsed that notion.[91]

---

[90]*Nezavisimaya Gazeta,* July 30, 1992 (FBIS-SOV, July 31, 1992, pp. 26–28). For the Russian military arguments, see pages 6–8 of this report. As noted earlier, despite the military's rhetoric, it is not clear to what extent the General Staff really believed that the southern Kurils remain indispensible to the defense of SSBNs in the Sea of Okhotsk. It should be noted, however, that the relative importance of those SSBNs will increase if the nuclear force reductions agreed on in the summer of 1992 are put into effect.

[91]Although there is less overt evidence, it seems likely that the hostile attitude toward a territorial settlement displayed by the Russian military leadership was matched by

The military broadside proved politically useful to the intransigents in the legislature, who vociferously sought to have Yeltsin cancel the Japan visit unless he and Kozyrev were prepared to guarantee in advance that they would make no concessions of any kind in Tokyo. Moreover, adamant nationalist positions opposing territorial concessions at this time were adopted not only by the conservative opposition, but also by some prominent legislators who favored internal reform, such as Oleg Rumyantsev, secretary of the constitutional commission of the Supreme Soviet, and Yevgeniy Ambartsumov, chairman of the legislature's International Affairs Committee. Not least important for Yeltsin was the fact that the Russian Supreme Soviet—and possibly a local referendum as well—would be required to confirm any settlement with Japan. In late August the International Affairs Committee reminded Yeltsin that under Russia's governing Federal Treaty, no section of the border could be changed without the consent of the relevant unit of the Russian Federation—in this case, Sakhalin oblast.[92]

Although until the last minute Yeltsin resisted the pressure for cancellation, he was driven in the end to yield because the negotiations between Russia and Japan during the weeks leading up to the scheduled departure never did reach agreement on what was to be accomplished by the visit.

The Russian negotiators knew that it was now extremely doubtful that Yeltsin could get enough domestic backing if he were to grant the Japanese demand for recognition of "residual" Japanese sovereignty over all four islands—even if actual possession of the two biggest islands, Kunashiri and Etorofu, were left in Russian hands for

---

its Japanese counterpart. Although the Japan Defense Agency has acknowledged a reduction in the Russian threat, the agency is believed in many quarters to have had a vested interest in continuation of the impasse with Moscow, since it probably fears, rightly or wrongly, that any broad Russian-Japanese settlement would have negative budgetary implications for the agency and could weaken defense planning efforts. On the other hand, one must recognize that the Japanese military leadership plays a much weaker role in policy determination in Tokyo than the Russian military leadership does in Moscow.

[92]INTERFAX news service, August 25, 1992 (FBIS-SOV, August 26, 1992, pp. 9–10).

a long time.[93]   Moreover, even without that Russian concession about sovereignty, it was now also increasingly uncertain that he could get enough domestic support merely for a two-island deal reviving the Khrushchev 1956 proposal regarding Shikotan and the Habomais. Even moderates in parliament were warning that regardless of the legal merits of that limited concession, it would be unwise to offer it now because that would play into the hands of reactionaries hoping to destroy Yeltsin's entire program.   There was general agreement that, as parliament's International Affairs Committee put it, "under present circumstances" it would be "extremely dangerous" for him to recognize Japan's sovereignty over *"any* part of Russian territory."[94] (Emphasis added.)

In the Japanese elite, the pressure of emotions was almost as severe. The Japanese government saw itself as limited in its freedom of maneuver even if it had in principle been willing (which it was not) to consider yielding on the biggest sticking point with the Russians— the demand for Russian recognition of Japanese "residual sovereignty" over all the islands. The leadership believed that even if it had wished to drop this demand, the accumulated passions of the last two decades would have exacted a prohibitive domestic political price.

Some observers disagree with this judgment. The Soviet Union for many years, and some Western and Japanese critics more recently, have contended that Japanese public support for their government's intransigence about the Northern Territories is illusory and has been artificially conjured up by LDP conservatives. Such critics therefore suggest that the Foreign Ministry has more political room for flexibility on the Northern Territories issue than it professes to have. Recent polling data seem to give some support to this contention.[95]

---

[93]The Japanese were said to have initially told the Russians that transfer of these two larger islands should take place within four or five years after signing of a peace treaty, but this negotiating position was undoubtedly soft, and the timetable could have been significantly extended. Indeed, in August 1992 Japan is said to have offered to delay even the transfer of Shikotan and the Habomais for some time after a treaty was signed. *(Tokyo Shimbun,* August 16, 1992.)

[94]INTERFAX news service, August 25, 1992 (FBIS-SOV, August 26, 1992, pp. 9–10).

[95]After the cancellation of the Yeltsin visit, one newspaper poll suggested a fair amount of public support for a relaxation of the LDP dictum that economic aid to Russia must be be tied to settlement of the territorial issue. Although support for

However, that view may underestimate the residual popular distrust and dislike of Russia in Japan and to understate the degree to which the Japanese public's attitude has been conditioned over the years by the LDP's tough line.[96] Despite the fact that considerable conciliatory sentiment has indeed grown in recent years both inside and outside the LDP, it seems probable that those willing to give up insistence on the claim to sovereignty over all four of the Northern Territories are still a minority in Japan. Thus the LDP leadership over the years has probably indeed limited its own capacity to change policy rapidly and dramatically on the territorial issue without suffering what it fears would be grave political embarrassment.

But although the Japanese demands regarding the islands could not soon be altered, the other half of the Japanese position—Japan's refusal to specify the quid pro quo that Russia could expect in exchange for return of the islands—might have been radically changed without such adverse internal political repercussions. Tokyo declined, however, to do so. This event that did not happen was perhaps the most striking feature of the negotiations that preceded the scheduled Yeltsin visit. The Japanese governing elite remained unwilling to communicate privately to the Russian government a specific promise spelling out the scope and nature of the economic reward that would follow *if* the Japanese political demands regarding the Northern Territories were accepted.

It will be recalled that in March 1991, Japan had provided Soviet leaders with such explicit information, for the first and last time. On that occasion, then secretary-general of the LDP Ozawa had carried to Moscow for presentation to Gorbachev a $26 billion package which gave Moscow concrete information about a meaningful quid pro quo the Soviets might obtain in return for consent to Japanese

---

Japan's claim to all four Northern Territories seems very widespread, support for the government's tactics in pursuing the claim seems much more diffuse. (*Nihon Keizai Shimbun*, September 29, 1992.)

[96]One indirect indicator of the Japanese public's attitude up to now on this question is the position the Japanese Communist Party (JCP) has traditionally taken on the territorial quarrel with Russia—a position that has always been more extreme than that of the LDP. It may be presumed that the JCP in adopting this very hard line toward Russia has responded to its opportunistic sense of the direction of public sentiment.

terms on the Northern Territories.[97]   This package was ten times larger than the sum Tokyo has so far held out (but mostly not delivered) to Yeltsin in the absence of a territorial settlement.   As recounted earlier, Gorbachev by April 1991 was too weak to accept the relatively attractive offer that Ozawa presented.   But it is noteworthy that Tokyo was unwilling eighteen months later to communicate to Yeltsin, even unofficially and informally, the same quid pro quo it had offered Gorbachev.

Several factors may have contributed to this mysterious refusal to act.   Probably least important were the rhetorical assurances made by spokesmen of both Russia and Japan to their respective publics that the islands "were not for sale" and "could not be bought."   In fact, both sides well knew that some informal mutual understanding of the value to be exchanged would in the end be necessary if a settlement were ever to be reached, even if the quid pro quo could not be spelled out publicly *as such* in official documents because of mutual political sensitivities.[98]

More important was the lack of a strong impulse from the Japanese business community pressing the Japanese government to make such an offer.   In the 1970s, Japan had been motivated to enter into prolonged but unsuccessful efforts to secure access to large West Siberian oil deposits, but since then structural changes in the Japanese economy had reduced the urgency of Japanese need for alternative energy resources in Russia.   The poorly developed infrastructure of Siberia and the Far East and the high marginal costs of resource development have historically tended to discourage large investment by foreigners (and indeed, have slowed investment by Moscow itself).[99]   As Tsuyoshi Hasegawa has pointed out, prospects

---

[97]For details, see the last portion of Chapter Two above.

[98]To be sure, since the cancellation of the Yeltsin visit, few Russians are willing to admit the acceptability of direct linkage.   Even some who support territorial concessions to Japan now insist that "the straightforward linkage of economic aid with the territorial dispute is an insult to Russia" that would "compromise Russia's foreign policy." (Aleksei Arbatov and Boris Makeyev, "The Kuril Barrier," *New Times*, October 1992, pp. 24–25.) However, this rhetoric does not eliminate the fact that no mutual retreat from the present entrenched positions is likely without some tacit understanding about a quid pro quo.

[99]See Sumiye O. McGuire, *Soviet-Japanese Economic Relations*, RAND, R-3817, May 1990.

for increased Japanese trade and investment have traditionally been hindered by the structural fact that Japanese trade with the Russians has rested almost entirely in the hands of certain very large, risk-taking Japanese trading companies, for whom Russian trade has been a rather small component of their total trading interests. Consequently, there has been no significant lobby in the Japanese business community with a large individual stake in the Russian market.[100] And finally, of course, the political uncertainties created by the gradual disintegration of the Soviet state in Gorbachev's final years has been followed by the even greater political, economic, and financial difficulties associated with Yeltsin's wavering struggle to build a market economy. The net result has been to attenuate Japan's near-term economic interest in the benefits that might flow from a settlement with Russia, leaving Japan's political interest in securing the return of the Northern Territories as the primary prospective motive for making a sacrifice to secure a settlement.[101] Thus far, that motive has evidently not been enough.

Probably most important of all in explaining Japan's inaction were factional trends within the LDP. Recent Japanese political scandals had at least temporarily weakened the position of Ichiro Ozawa, the organizer of the 1991 offer to Gorbachev and the leading advocate of a revitalization of Japanese foreign policy. The Japanese Foreign Ministry, which has always preferred to reserve its position on the rewards that would flow to Russia in exchange for return of the is-

---

[100]Tsuyoshi Hasegawa, "Soviet-Japanese Relations in the 1990s," *Far Eastern Affairs* (Moscow), No. 2, 1991. In contrast, Hasegawa notes, Japanese trade and investment with such Western countries as Germany and America, in addition to being larger, are far more broadly spread among Japanese corporations, creating a much stronger set of vested interests.

[101]Arbatov and Makeyev (fn. 98) acknowledge that the present economic and political situation in Russia deters Japanese investment, and argue that consequently, "more radical reforms in Russia, financial stability, and every encouragement of foreign investments" must precede Russian-Japanese normalization. While rejecting the possibility of a Japanese economic quid pro quo for Russian territorial concessions, these authors in effect argue that limited unilateral Russian concessions, coupled with radical economic reforms, would lead the Japanese into large-scale economic cooperation with Russia. Although these arguments have some weight, the difficulty with them is that without politically driven Japanese transitional help, the internal Russian changes Arbatov and Makeyev posit may never occur on the scale required. The Russian writers would in effect abandon the possibility that in exchange for a territorial settlement, Russia could obtain the aid of the Japanese government in bridging the gap to radical Russian reform.

lands, was unhappy when momentarily compelled by the LDP to abandon that stance in March 1991, and saw that event as an aberration it did not wish to repeat.   In the absence of a situation that would allow concerted LDP pressure once more to be focused on the Foreign Ministry, the Ozawa offer could not be resurrected. In addition, the fact that the 1991 offer had been rejected, and the considerable possibility that Yeltsin might also feel obliged to do so,[102] no doubt contributed to the elite's disinclination to try again. Finally, as already noted, some Japanese officials had warned in the spring of 1992, when Japan was compelled by its Western partners to join in funding for Russia through international channels, that Japan might compensate itself by restricting what it did for Russia through bilateral channels.

During the pre-summit negotiations, Russia apparently sought without success to prod Japan into specifying its hypothetical economic quid pro quo. After the Yeltsin visit was cancelled, an unidentified senior government source in Tokyo disclosed that the Russian side had made "an informal request" for $50 billion in long-term aid from Japan. The senior source explained that Japan of course had rejected this request, since without a territorial settlement "there is no way we could respond to Russia's wish for $50 billion."[103]   The Japanese official did not explain, however, why Japan had not chosen to make a counteroffer conditional on acceptance of its terms for the Northern Territories. It seems likely that the enormous sum put forward "informally" by the Russians was intended to elicit such a hypothetical counteroffer.

---

[102]Although the Russian response even to a renewal of the very large Ozawa offer would have been problematical at best, some prominent officials of the Russian legislature who were opposed to territorial concessions under existing circumstances have privately stated that a massive Japanese economic offer might have made a difference. (Private conversation.)

[103]KYODO, September 10, 1992 (FBIS-EAS, September 10, 1992, p. 9). The figure of $50 billion apparently derived from an unpublished proposal, conveyed by a trilateral academic group to the governments of Russia, Japan, and the United States in August 1992. This proposal suggested, among other things, that Japan help resolve the dispute by agreeing to provide $5 billion to Russia annually for ten years. After receipt of the proposal, Russian officials apparently followed it up with informal inquiries to Tokyo, with negative results.

A more serious and "formal" Russian request, apparently predicated on the assumption that there would be no breakthrough on the territorial issue, was for a package including some $1.5 to $2 billion for crude oil and natural gas projects,[104] commitments for help on 12 high-technology priority projects including optical communications and peaceful uses of nuclear materials,[105] and the signing of treaties on investment protection and economic cooperation intended to minimize risks from foreign investments and thus encourage Japanese investment in Russia.[106]

The Japanese government's response to this list of requests was not flatly negative, but it was minimal. The proposed treaties on investment protection were dismissed out of hand, since Tokyo was unwilling to open the door for widespread Japanese investment in Russia in the absence of a territorial settlement. Vice Premier Shokhin also apparently obtained little encouragement regarding a new Japanese credit package specifically targeted either for oil and gas development or for his 12 key high-technology projects. Instead, the Japanese insisted that any assistance they did eventually decide to furnish for any of these purposes would have to be subtracted from the $1.8 billion pool of export insurance that was supposedly set aside for Russia in October 1991—nearly a year earlier—but which Japan had mostly not yet allowed to be put into effect "because of the country's declining credit-worthiness" (i.e., because Russia could not pay its old debts, and was in fact seeking a long-term debt moratorium).[107]   However, Tokyo was now willing to

---

[104]This request was highlighted by Deputy Premier Aleksandr Shokhin in a Moscow press conference in late August. (KYODO, August 29, 1992, FBIS-SOV, August 31, 1992, p. 7.) The 12 priority projects were apparently part of a more amorphous total of some 150 projects on which Japanese cooperation was sought by various segments of the Russian government.

[105]Russian Deputy Premier Poltoranin is said to have sounded out Japan on these projects during a visit to Japan in early August. (*Sankei Shimbun*, September 6, 1992.)

[106]*Nihon Keizai Shimbun*, August 25, 1992.

[107]KYODO, August 29, 1992 (FBIS-EAS, August 31, 1992). By mid-September 1992, Japanese trading houses faced $1.36 billion in delayed payments for exports made to the former Soviet Union. The payment delays were said to have started in the autumn of 1989, and to have gradually risen ever since, with some payment deadlines missed on even some bank-guaranteed contracts. (KYODO, September 14, 1992 [FBIS-EAS, September 16, 1992, p. 1].) A similar situation existed with Russian debts to other major industrial countries, and throughout 1992 Russia had obtained from the West a

release from this pool of prospective trade insurance $700 million to finance Japanese machinery sales to increase Russian gas production, satisfying that part of Shokhin's request.[108] In addition, Japan was now at last prepared to release the $100 million in humanitarian assistance first pledged to the Soviet Union as long ago as December 1990 but never delivered.[109] Finally, Japan was also willing to supply a token $25 million to promote the safety of the nuclear power industry. These three funding commitments—almost entirely flowing from old pledges—were represented as Japan's contribution to the bilateral assistance portion of the international package pledged to Russia by the G-7 in the spring of 1992.

Japanese political strategy for dealing with Yeltsin at the summit was formulated against the background of these firm decisions on the limits of bilateral economic assistance. Tokyo was well aware that Yeltsin would find it impossible to acknowledge Japanese sovereignty over all four islands. But the Japanese government afterward said it had hoped that Yeltsin would nevertheless have found it possible—in return for the very limited economic package just described—to

---

series of short-term moratoria on debt repayment, which it vainly sought to get its creditors to replace with a long-term moratorium.

[108]In so doing, Japan was also fulfilling a promise to release credits in this amount which Miyazawa had apparently made at the Munich G-7 meeting in July. (*Nihon Keizai Shimbun*, September 18, 1992.)

[109]One Japanese newspaper asserted that this $100 million in help had been held up by disagreement as to how to divide it among the former Soviet republics, and that Japan would now deliver the assistance under an agreement whereby the Russian Foreign Trade Bank would coordinate the distribution among the republics. (*Yomiuri Shimbun*, August 24, 1992.) This explanation for the delay seems inadequate. Indeed, after the cancellation of the Yeltsin visit, Premier Miyazawa acknowledged that bureaucratic procrastination and obstruction in Tokyo bore at least some of the responsibility. He said that "I should take the blame for taking more than a year to work out a $100 million grant to Russia," adding that the current government procedures for deciding on Russian aid were too time-consuming because they required Miyazawa to obtain support from four concerned ministries. (*Nihon Keizai Shimbun*, September 17, 1992.) It seems possible that the Finance Ministry, once again, was a leading recalcitrant.

Subsequently, at an international conference on aid to the former Soviet states held in Tokyo in October 1992, Japan announced that the $100 million would be furnished as a grant rather than as a loan (as originally described 22 months earlier). Some 60 percent of the help would go to Russia (mostly to the Russian Far East), with the rest being distributed to other former Soviet republics. (ITAR-TASS, October 29, 1992 [FBIS-SOV, October 30, 1992].)

reaffirm the validity of the 1956 agreement pledging return of two islands while agreeing to continue talks on the other two.[110]

The Russian Foreign Ministry and the political forces allied with the ministry were willing to do this, but it should have been obvious to Tokyo that these Russian forces were increasingly outgunned. In early August, the moderate Vice Premier Mikhail Poltoranin visited Japan, journeyed to Okinawa, and expressed interest in a solution for the territorial problem modeled on America's arrangement with Japan over Okinawa—meaning that Russia would recognize Japan's "residual sovereignty" over the Northern Territories, but would be allowed to retain its military facilities on the islands indefinitely. Although ingeniously designed to bypass Russian military opposition to a territorial deal, this suggestion was unacceptable to Japan, and probably also to many Russians as well.[111] Poltoranin and some Russian Foreign Ministry officials also toyed publicly with the notion of referring the dispute to the International Court of Justice, but dominant forces in both countries seemed to remain opposed to such a proposal.[112]

---

[110]Statement attributed to Foreign Minister Watanabe in the immediate aftermath of the visit's cancellation. (KYODO, September 11, 1992.) This was in fact the proposal Watanabe is said to have put to the Russians during his preparatory visit to Moscow in late August. Another view holds that the real and more modest Japanese goal was merely to "make sure that Yeltsin said nothing to contradict the 1956 Soviet statement offering to return two of the islands, while leaving open the final status of the other two islands." In return, Yeltsin would have obtained, in lieu of more economic help from Japan, a better atmosphere for future international discussions about help. (*Washington Post,* September 17, 1992.)

[111]Japan was most unlikely to accept a settlement legitimizing continued Russian military presence on the Northern Territories. Many Russian nationalists, on the other hand, would reject such a deal if a prerequisite was Russian recognition of Japanese residual sovereignty over the islands.

[112]The decisive factor on the Russian side would be nationalist resistance to the notion of allowing any third party to decide the fate of territory now under Russian control; and on the Japanese side, by evident misgivings about the strength of the Japanese legal case. Various other compromise alternatives for a territorial settlement have been put forward by different observers in recent years. For example, one Russian scholar has proposed adopting the New Hebrides solution of 1906 whereby Britain and France opted to jointly administer those disputed islands, while some in the West have suggested a United Nations trusteeship for the southern Kurils. Some such suggestions were no doubt included in the list of settlement "variants" which Yeltsin had been prepared to carry to Tokyo. If ever officially advanced in negotiations, almost any such compromise proposal, no matter how reasonable in appear-

In mid-August, Yeltsin told a Japanese television audience that during his visit to Japan he was prepared to sign an agreement to withdraw all Russian forces from the southern Kurils by mid-1995.[113] He observed that this withdrawal would constitute fulfillment of the third stage of the five-stage plan he had put forward in January 1990, and said the fourth stage would involve signing a bilateral peace treaty. He continued to insist that solution of the territorial question could only come as the fifth and final stage, after the signing of a treaty. Yeltsin asserted that Russia had prepared more than ten alternatives for consideration concerning this final, territorial stage.[114] Obviously, however, all these Russian "variants" were irrelevant if the Japanese continued to insist that a treaty must follow a territorial agreement, and thus rejected Yeltsin's proposed line of march toward an agreement.

By late August, when Yeltsin's chief of staff Yuriy Petrov was sent to Tokyo for further conversations with the Japanese, Petrov's sour comments made it apparent that Yeltsin's expectations for the visit had further declined. From Yeltsin's perspective, unless he accepted the enormous political risks involved in a territorial settlement on Japanese terms, the Japanese would neither sign a peace treaty nor grant the Russian economic wish list put forward by Vice Premier Shokhin. Yet at the same time, Japan could not be enticed into volunteering reliable information as to the scope of the economic reward Yeltsin could expect if he did accept a territorial settlement on Japanese terms. Nor, apparently, was the Japanese position appreciably affected by Yeltsin's promise to sign an agreement to demilitarize the southern Kurils, a unilateral concession that Japan evi-

---

ance to the outside observer, would under present circumstances face severe resistance from nationalist forces on one side or the other, and often from both.

[113]KYODO, August 17, 1992 (FBIS-SOV, August 17, 1992, p. 6). This was a somewhat longer period than Yeltsin had indicated to Foreign Minister Watanabe in May, when he had said that all forces on the four islands would be completely removed "within one or two years." As noted earlier, Defense Minister Grachev had publicly contradicted that statement. Yeltsin now said that he had arrived at his new estimate after consultation with Grachev. Two weeks later, Yeltsin added that "we are prepared to do this but we seek an understanding with Japan," implying that Yeltsin meant the agreement on demilitarization of the islands to be part of a deal involving unspecified concessions on the Japanese side, perhaps regarding economic aid, or perhaps involving Japanese agreement to sign a peace treaty prior to a territorial settlement.

[114]ITAR-TASS, August 17, 1992.

dently intended to pocket without additional early recompense. On the other hand, Russia had good reason to believe that because of Western pressure on Japan, those limited economic investment and assistance measures Japan had already arranged for the summit would be forthcoming whether the summit took place or not—as indeed subsequently proved to be the case.

In early September, when Foreign Minister Watanabe visited Moscow to make final preparations for the summit, Yeltsin astonished Watanabe by declining to discuss details of the territorial question with him, saying that he would make his position on that issue clear only to Premier Miyazawa during the summit.   This stonewalling by Yeltsin was widely seen as extraordinary, not only because it brought to a halt preparation of the most important aspect of the summit documents, but also because Yeltsin's statement was regarded in Japan as a personal insult to Watanabe (and not the first such insult).[115] At the same time, however, it is equally important to note that Watanabe was also stonewalling. There is reason to believe that Yeltsin had hoped that Watanabe would carry with him to Moscow some information regarding the economic quid pro quo that Japan would provide to Russia in connection with a territorial settlement. But nothing of this kind was forthcoming.

On the whole, it is likely that Yeltsin's unfortunate treatment of Watanabe was a by-product of his genuine indecision about how to resolve the dilemma in which he had been placed. To proceed with the visit to Japan and there formally endorse only Khrushchev's two-island concession, while leaving the fate of the other two islands open—as Japan hoped he would do and his Foreign Ministry wished him to do—was to accept major adverse domestic political consequences while still failing to secure an early peace treaty, a territorial settlement, or a specific big new Japanese economic reward. To go to Tokyo and leave with little to show for it but continued stalemate on the territorial issue was to invite comparison with the weak Gorbachev and Gorbachev's futile 1991 visit. But to cancel the visit outright was to give comfort to his domestic political enemies who had long sought to compel him to take that action.

---

[115]It will be recalled that in January 1992, Yeltsin had failed to keep an appointment to meet with Watanabe in Moscow.

In the end, after hesitating until the last minute, Yeltsin concluded that aborting the visit involved the smallest losses. Although as late as September 5 he evidently was still planning to go through with the journey,[116] four days later he phoned Miyazawa to inform him of the cancellation. This act had predictable consequences. As expected, Russian conservative and ultranationalist forces—both in the parliamentary opposition and within Yeltsin's own apparatus—were triumphant, whereas the Foreign Ministry and the progressive minority who supported it were bitter and dismayed.[117] In Tokyo, there was considerable anger in the government and the LDP not only about the last-minute cancellation itself, but also about the rhetoric that soon emerged in Moscow blaming the cancellation on Japan, which encouraged some Japanese public criticism of the Miyazawa government's handling of the negotiations. The recriminations now heard on both sides suggested that underlying tensions between the dominant forces in the two elites had considerably worsened, and that progress toward a settlement would be further delayed.

Although diplomatic contacts between Russia and Japan were soon resumed and both sides joined in attempting to limit the damage, it seems evident that a watershed was passed with the collapse of plans for the Yeltsin visit. The cancellation brought to a dismal climax the phase in the Russo-Japanese relationship that had begun so hopefully a year earlier in the aftermath of Yeltsin's triumph over the coup plotters. The expectations of an early rapprochement that emerged when Yeltsin took power were now definitely gone, along with hopes that a massive infusion of Japanese capital would soon arrive in

---

[116]On September 5 Yeltsin recorded an interview for Japanese television and said that in spite of Japanese "hysteria" over the Northern Territories issue, "I am not refusing to visit; the visit will take place." (FBIS-SOV, September 8, 1992, p. 7.)

[117]Kozyrev subsequently blamed members of the presidential "apparatus" for having "interfered in foreign policy" and having helped to kill the visit. This seemed an allusion to the subordinates of Yeltsin's chief of staff Petrov. Kozyrev also alluded caustically to the negative effect of a public statement issued by the presidential security service on September 3 casting doubt on Japan's ability to guarantee Yeltsin's safety. He implied that this statement had been generated within Petrov's "apparatus" without Yeltsin's approval to impel Yeltsin toward cancellation of the visit. (*Moskovskiy Novosty,* No. 38, September 20, 1992.)

Russia to make a decisive difference in Russia's internal economic and political struggle. We now turn to the implications of this new reality for the future of America's relationship with Japan.

Chapter Four

IMPLICATIONS FOR U.S.-JAPAN RELATIONS

THE U.S. DILEMMA OVER JAPAN AND RUSSIA

The cancellation of the Yeltsin visit not only dramatized to the world the gravity of the impasse between Russia and Japan, but also brought into focus a dilemma of American policy that had been growing ever since the failure of the August 1991 Moscow coup. This dilemma arose because of the conflict between two important American interests. One was the vested interest in the survival of a moderate, stable, and democratic government in Russia, friendly to the West, rejecting the expansionist, militarist impulses of the past, yet firmly in control of its nuclear weapons. The other was the U.S. interest in the preservation of the military alliance with Japan, until recently predicated on common hostility to Moscow, as a fundamental bulwark of the overall Japanese-American relationship. Both interests are now under threat—the first right now, the other over the next decade. The dilemma for the United States is sharpened by the fact that the evolution of events is forcing Washington for the first time to confront choices between these two sets of interests.

RUSSIAN PROSPECTS AND THE WASHINGTON-TOKYO ALLIANCE

There seems little doubt that the outlook for the Yeltsin regime is grave, and that it was worsened by the September 1992 debacle with Japan. This fact has already created a new kind of American friction with Japan, superimposed on the existing economic frictions. We have seen that in the spring of 1992 the United States saw itself compelled to split with the political interests of its Japanese ally because of its own perceived stake in Russian stability. This was by no means the first time the United States had opposed an important Japanese interest, but it was certainly the first time since World War II that it had been done to help Moscow.

When the United States shifted away from the Japanese side in the G-7 discussions, thus reducing Japanese bargaining leverage with Russia over the Northern Territories, it dramatized to the Japanese elite a fact they already knew in the abstract, that the old rationale for the Japanese-American alliance had already greatly eroded. Nothing has yet taken its place, so that the alliance is being sustained by inertia. There is a widening contrast between the new relationship that America and other Western states have sought to build with post–cold war Russia, on the one hand, and Japan's icy relations with Russia, on the other. Although Japanese leaders wish to minimize the extent of this difference, they seem unlikely over the next year or two to retreat in order to eliminate it.

The Japanese government is thus likely over the near term to adhere to its doctrine of tight linkage between politics (the territorial issue) and economics (major Japanese economic help for Russia). To be sure, some gaps have developed in the enforcement of this doctrine, but on the whole it is still intact. The biggest breach was created by the action of the G-7 states in compelling Japan to begin to furnish funds to Russia through joint international channels. In addition, there has been considerable small-scale Japanese investment activity in the Russian Far East, as well as the recent larger agreement to fund sales to the Russian gas industry. But on the whole, Japanese money is not flowing to Russia on a scale remotely relevant to the scope of Russian economic needs, largely because the risks associated with investment in the chaotic Russian polity and economy have grown increasingly incommensurate with the prospective rewards. Only very large-scale, politically motivated financial guarantees from the Japanese government can change this pattern, and under present circumstances change on this scale seems quite unlikely.

Meanwhile, Japan remains the key to Russian hopes for a revitalized relationship with East Asia, which for several decades has been the most dynamic region of the world economy. Despite much recent talk in some sectors of the Russian press about a need to shift the emphasis of foreign policy toward greater cultivation of the East, it seems unlikely that such a shift will be fruitful without a Russian modus vivendi with the dominant East Asian economy.[1]

Some in Moscow have evidently placed hope in the possibility of securing substitutes elsewhere in Asia for Japanese loans and investments, pointing particularly to the economic benefits to be expected from expanded relations with the Republic of Korea and, to a lesser extent, with China, Hong Kong, Singapore, and Taiwan. For several years, the Soviet Union and Russia have sought to exploit the unfolding relationship with South Korea—spurred by Seoul's political interest in using Moscow against Pyongyang—as an instrument of leverage on Japan. Yeltsin was therefore at pains, when he cancelled his visit to Tokyo in September 1992, to make clear that he wished to go ahead with an early visit to Seoul.   This visit occurred in November, and Seoul then agreed to resume the second half of a credit package suspended for nearly a year because of past Russian failure to pay interest on existing credits.[2]

Yet it seems improbable, in view of Russian economic realities and Russian difficulty in servicing debts, that either Korean resources available for Russia or Korean enthusiasm for investment in Russia will exist at a level sufficient to make an important difference.[3]

---

[1]Some Russians acknowledge this fundamental reality. "Without Japan—the world's leading exporter of capital—it is impossible to create a modern market infrastructure in the Far East. Without it, no major deals will be made with South Korea, Taiwan, Hongkong and Singapore." (Alexei Arbatov and Boris Makeyev, "The Kuril Barrier," *New Times*, October 1992, pp. 24–26.) A similar view was expressed by Konstantin Eggert in *Izvestiya*, September 15, 1992.

[2]As earlier noted, in January 1991, in tacit exchange for Gorbachev's establishment of diplomatic relations with the Republic of Korea the previous September, Seoul had formally agreed to a $3 billion package of loans and credits to help Moscow buy Korean products. In December, after about half of this aid money had been disbursed, South Korea halted the program because Russia had failed to pay interest on the loans. The second $1.5 billion tranche of Korean credits was released on the eve of Yeltsin's November 1992 visit when Russia agreed to pay past interest due. *(New York Times, November 18, 1992.)* It is evident that Yeltsin made great efforts to secure the internal funds and commodities needed for this purpose, in part because of his hope that resumption of the Korean credit program—and ostentatious display of a warm relationship with South Korea—would put pressure on Japan.

[3]See accounts in *New York Times*, November 18, 1992, and *Financial Times*, November 21–22, 1992.

China, on the other hand, is a valuable customer for Russian military hardware and a useful supplier of food and textiles, but cannot be a major source of investment funds or advanced technology. The conclusion remains that unless and until there is a breakthrough with Japan, Russia will not become decisively engaged with East Asia.

A final consideration on this subject is that a clock is ticking. There is reason to believe that the large Japanese pool of surplus investment capital that might potentially be made available to Russia will not remain available for many years. After the middle of the decade, these surplus investment funds may diminish rapidly because of sharply rising alternative demands for investment already on the horizon, especially for huge planned Japanese domestic investment and major scheduled increases in investment and assistance in Asia.[4] The window of opportunity for a mutually profitable territorial settlement is thus limited.

IF YELTSIN FALLS: RECRIMINATIONS OVER "WHO LOST RUSSIA?"

The net conclusion is that if Yeltsin and his reform program are to revive in the face of the present crisis, that will have to be accomplished without a Japanese lifeline. But there is a substantial possibility that neither Yeltsin nor his program will, in fact, long survive, and that Yeltsin may lose power entirely in the next year or two, to be replaced by a more conservative, highly nationalist regime, not only less oriented toward the market but also less friendly to the West.

Throughout 1992, an increasingly plausible alternative to Yeltsin's outright replacement was that Yeltsin would manage to hold on to his title as President, but only at the cost of yielding on a much broader front than before to the demands of an increasingly conservative and chauvinist opposition. Such a massive retreat by Yeltsin could involve virtual if not explicit abandonment of his present halting, inconsistent, and painful efforts to move Russia toward a market system. It could mean much greater integration of key conservative figures from the old Soviet regime into Yeltsin's administration, and

---

[4]I am indebted to Charles Wolf, Jr. and Vladimir Shkolnikov for their insights on this issue.

much greater concessions to the demands of a Russian military institution increasingly oriented along the lines of its Soviet predecessor. It could imply the acceleration of forcible efforts to reassert Russian influence and consolidate Russian presence in outlying parts of the old Soviet Union. And finally, it could mean a much sharper turn toward the pursuit of external Russian national interests as they are interpreted by Russian conservatives, at the expense of the tendency to cooperate with the United States and the West.

During 1992 there was a significant growth of pressures on Yeltsin to retreat on all of these fronts, to which he responded with big concessions in some areas and strong resistance in others. The cancellation of Yeltsin's visit to Japan was one of the retreats in question.[5] By the close of the year, he had finally yielded to reactionary pressure at the December 1992 Congress of People's Deputies and had abandoned the Gaidar government. It remained to be seen how far this most drastic retreat would carry him, and to what extent the tendency toward internal reform and external moderation could survive.

If, in the end, Yeltsin either falls or becomes a total prisoner of the right, there will probably be many recriminations to follow, both inside the United States and other Western countries and between the United States and its allies. Despite the fact that the United States has itself been unwilling to make substantial sacrifices to assist Russia, Japan—because of its greater potential to help—is widely, and with some justice, regarded as the leading recalcitrant. The Japanese therefore have reason to believe that a political disaster in Moscow would trigger a widespread tendency in the West to blame Japan.

In a superficial sense, such a disastrous change in Moscow's total orientation could be seen as simplifying Japan's problem in dealing with the United States and Western Europe over the Russian issue. The emergence of a Russian government no longer committed to economic transformation would discourage continuation of the IMF/World Bank rescue effort, in principle eliminating that source of Japanese-American strain. And the advent of a hard-line Russian

---

[5]Among many other such partial Yeltsin retreats was his announcement in the fall of 1992 of at least temporary suspension of the military withdrawal from Latvia and Estonia, despite his promise to the contrary at the G-7 summit in July.

regime dominated by a military-conservative coalition and markedly less friendly to the United States on a broad spectrum of issues would presumably narrow the present gap between U.S. and Japanese attitudes toward Moscow, to that extent easing the tensions caused by Japanese intransigence over the Northern Territories.

It is improbable, however, that many in the Japanese elite are hoping for an outright triumph of Russian reactionaries, or believe it would really solve the problems facing the Japanese-American alliance. Despite Japan's continuing territorial quarrel with Russia, most Japanese are well aware that they, like the Europeans and the Americans, have benefited from the demise of the militarized Soviet state, particularly because of the great reduction in the military threat posed by that state to neighboring Japan. They have little reason to welcome the coming to power of men who could well prove more hostile to Japan than Yeltsin. Moreover, the Japanese have no less reason than others to fear that Yeltsin's fall might presage eventual chaos in Russia and possible loss of central control over nuclear weapons.

Finally, the advent of a Russian government markedly less inclined to cooperate with the United States would not eliminate the American domestic budgetary pressures for reduction of the U.S. force posture in the western Pacific. Nor would the emergence of an unfriendly regime in Moscow revive Moscow's vanished capability to mount a worldwide challenge to the United States, since the massive decline in Russian military capabilities has stemmed from catastrophic economic and geopolitical changes that will not disappear even if Yeltsin does. No change in leadership—or leadership attitudes—in Moscow can restore Russia as a global superpower for many years, and the bipolar world will not soon return. Consequently, the American sense of an overarching struggle with an implacable global opponent, the fundamental factor that justified the Japanese alliance to the American public for forty years, will not be available in the present decade no matter what happens in Moscow. Thus, any in the Japanese elite who did expect the old rationale for the Japanese-American alliance to be revived by adverse trends in Russia would probably be proved mistaken. Meanwhile, however, the search for a new rationale for the alliance would be delayed.

IF YELTSIN "MUDDLES ALONG": THE ISSUE OF U.S. INVOLVEMENT

Alternatively, there is some chance that despite the fall of Gaidar, the Yeltsin regime will go on "muddling through" over the next few years with overall trends in the country substantially unchanged. Under this scenario, the Russian government will continue to lean to some degree toward cooperation with the United States, but will also continue to be constrained from making the concessions to Japan needed for a territorial settlement. Yeltsin, according to this hypothesis, will continue to walk a tightrope on economic policy, maneuvering between the urgings of the West on one side to press ahead with marketization and the pressure from his industrial lobby on the other side to slow it down. He will make barely enough concessions to IMF demands to keep a flow of capital coming through international channels sufficient to underwrite a minimum of imports and investments from the West. But economic progress and prospects in Russia will remain very poor, and this will be attributed by many in Russia to a lack of sufficient Western—and especially Japanese—help.

Under these circumstances, bitter Russian attacks on the Japanese for their footdragging are likely to emerge more frequently and openly. More important for the United States and the future of its alliance with Japan is the fact that efforts to involve America directly in the Russian-Japanese dispute may surface more often.

On the one hand, we will probably hear some in Moscow more vigorously press the argument that the main obstacle to return of the southern Kurils is the Russian sense of threat from the U.S. force structure in the area, coupled with the existence of the U.S. military alliance with Japan. This argument, driven by the hope to weaken the alliance, was for a long time a staple of traditional Soviet foreign policy, but in recent years many Russians—and indeed, some military leaders—have come to recognize that the U.S.-Japan security treaty is consistent with Russian security interests because it serves to reduce the possibility of a growth in Japanese militarism and unconstrained rearmament. Consequently, talk about the American-Japanese security threat in the Far East had been heard only rarely in Yeltsin's Moscow until the summer of 1992. At that point, however, the Russian General Staff, in its written presentation to the legislature opposing return of the southern Kurils, justified its stance in precisely these terms, citing explicitly its supposed concerns about a potential U.S.-Japanese threat in the area.[6]

It is significant that a complementary line of argument has also begun to emerge from the opposing side of the Russian internal debate. The moderate former Russian Vice Premier Poltoranin, during his early August 1992 visit to Japan, not only suggested that the American base agreement with Japan could serve as a model for a Russian-Japanese agreement about the Kurils, but also hinted that the inverse was also true: that a reduction in the U.S. base presence in Okinawa and in Japan generally could facilitate Russian consent to demilitarize the southern Kurils.[7] Poltoranin also said that he favored direct U.S. "participation in the discussion of military problems linked with the South Kurils issue."[8] This contention has been echoed by Russian academics such as Konstantin Sarkisov, who have called on the United States to join in negotiations so as to help provide Russia with "safer borders" in northeast Asia.[9] If the economic deterioration in Russia and the impasse with Japan continue side by side, Japan and the United States may hear more overt appeals from Yeltsin's supporters alleging that the scope of the U.S. military presence tied to the alliance is anachronistic and plays into the hands of the Russian military leaders who have helped to block a deal with Japan.[10]

---

[6]*Nezavisimaya Gazeta*, July 30, 1992 (FBIS-SOV, July 31, 1992, pp. 26–28). It is not clear how far the General Staff officials who prepared this document believed what they wrote. Nevertheless, the alarmist and anachronistic view formally expressed by the General Staff remains politically potent in the present Moscow atmosphere.

[7]Poltoranin suggested that unilateral reductions of U.S. forces in Japan, and especially in Okinawa, are now appropriate; but "if Washington and Tokyo do not want these forces to leave," then they should accept the idea of long-term Russian base arrangements in the southern Kurils by analogy with the U.S. arrangement in Okinawa. (ITAR-TASS, August 6, 1992 [FBIS-SOV, August 7, 1992, p. 21].)

[8]ITAR-TASS, August 5, 1992 (FBIS-SOV, August 6, 1992, p. 15).

[9]Konstantin Sarkisov, "The Kurils—Pandora's Box?" *Moscow News*, August 9–16, 1992. It should be noted that Sarkisov, a leading Russian advocate of a territorial settlement with Japan, has been closely involved with American academics in work on the problem.

[10]This argument is likely to be pressed with the United States despite the fact that the Russian government will probably continue to find it difficult to promise return of all four disputed islands *even if* the supposed worries of the Russian military about the Japanese-American alliance were some day to be satisfied. Opposition in Russia to re-

In Japan, the government might be embarrassed if its own public ever came to perceive the U.S. force structure in the area and the American military relationship with Japan as the *only* big obstacle to Japan's retrieval of the Northern Territories. It is highly unlikely that this consideration would destroy the strong Japanese elite consensus in support of the alliance. In the United States, however, the situation is different, and ongoing domestic trends could generate a more significant response over the next few years to vigorous Russian appeals for major force reductions in the area, or even for some loosening of the security relationship with Japan.

Given the disappearance of the former Soviet Union's worldwide challenge to the United States and the growth of America's long-term economic difficulties and budget dilemmas, such Russian appeals may well find a response in many sectors of American opinion that would have been impossible in the days of Brezhnev and Andropov. This tendency in the United States could survive the disappearance of Premier Gaidar. Indeed, it is noteworthy that even before the cancellation of the September 1992 Yeltsin visit to Japan, some influential American voices had already begun to suggest that much greater U.S. force reductions were needed in the western Pacific—and not only to save money, but also to facilitate a Russo-Japanese territorial settlement.[11] It is likely that if Yeltsin survives, more such voices will be heard, in Congress as well as in the press.

In addition, some in the United States have already suggested that Washington should play a direct role in seeking to mediate the territorial issue.[12] Because of the importance the United States attaches

---

turn of the Northern Territories is not, in practice, limited to security concerns, but is much broader in nature, reflecting a visceral and emotional nationalism in much of the civilian population.

[11] Editorial in *New York Times*, August 28, 1992.

[12] See editorial in *Washington Post*, September 15, 1992, citing recommendations of "a group of Russian, Japanese and American scholars whose American chairman is Harvard's Graham Allison." These recommendations, prepared under the joint direction of Graham Allison, Hiroshi Kimura, and Konstantin Sarkisov, were published at the close of the year under the title *Beyond Cold War to Trilateral Cooperation in the Asia-Pacific Region: Scenarios for New Relationships Between Japan, Russia, and the United States* (Harvard University, Strengthening Democratic Institutions Project, Cambridge, Massachusetts, 1992). For the personal views of one participant in this project, see Peter Berton, *The Japanese-Russian Territorial Dilemma: Historical Back-*

to maintaining stability in Russia, the United States has already sought to encourage both sides toward mutual compromise, with little result. There are indeed good reasons why more vigorous and sustained intervention into this matter by the new U.S. administration could prove to be in the interests of all three countries. In this connection, a close coordination of America's Russia policy and America's Japan policy will be critical.

It is essential, however, that intervention be conducted with due regard for the American stake in preserving the alliance with Japan. While much greater concessions by both Japan and Russia will be required, the United States cannot afford to adopt a posture of complete neutrality on all the issues at stake. Thus the United States would incur significant political risks if, in the interests of mediation, it were to repudiate the posture of support for the Japanese territorial claims that America has maintained up to now. Such a radical shift would come as a shock, and seem a grievous betrayal to many Japanese.[13] Moreover, such a traumatic change would be particularly unfortunate because many Japanese believe that it was the United States—in the person of former Secretary of State John Foster Dulles—that had impelled Japan in the first place to turn away from the notion of a two-island settlement at a time, back in 1956, when Japanese leaders were considering accepting such a formula and Japanese public opinion had not yet hardened against it.[14]

---

ground, Disputes, Issues, Questions, Solution Scenarios (Harvard University, Strengthening Democratic Institutions Project, Cambridge, Massachusetts, 1992).

[13]There is in this connection a useful historical precedent in the American experience in promoting the Treaty of Portsmouth early in this century, when many Japanese tended to blame the United States for pressing on Japan a treaty settlement with Russia which, in their view, deprived them of many of the rightful fruits of their victory in the 1905 Russo-Japanese war. Although that resentment has long been superceded by subsequent events, a repetition would hardly be helpful for the relationship.

[14]Dulles at the time contended that if Japan formally recognized Soviet sovereignty over Kunashiri and Etorofu in order to accept the two-island deal offered by Khrushchev as the basis for a Soviet peace treaty, that would violate a clause of the 1951 San Francisco treaty (signed by America and Japan but not the Soviet Union) guaranteeing that the United States would in no respect receive worse terms than did the Soviet Union in any future treaty Tokyo signed with Moscow. Dulles therefore threatened to revoke American recognition of Japanese "residual sovereignty" over Okinawa if Japan took this step, and the Japanese leadership yielded to this pressure. Subsequently, the issue raised by the United States became moot, as a strong Japanese consensus emerged insisting on recovery of all four islands.

This does not mean, however, that the United States should remain passive toward its Russian-Japanese dilemma. One aspect of the problem that should get much greater U.S. attention has already been highlighted: the unwillingness of the Japanese governing elite to specify the economic recompense it would deliver to Russia in exchange for satisfaction of its territorial demands. This reticence seems to be grounded in more than tactical considerations. It suggests a certain doubt that recovery of the Northern Territories is, in fact, important enough to be worth a large Japanese economic sacrifice. It also implies some complacency about the status quo, as the result of an unstated vague assumption that the continuation of tensions with Russia somehow serves to postpone new problems for the military alliance with America. Many in the Japanese elite probably do not share these attitudes, but the ascendancy of those who do appears to be preserved by the nature of the LDP factional system and the intractibility of the Japanese decisionmaking process.

However, the assumption that Japan and the United States can indefinitely preserve the political foundations of their alliance while ignoring their diverging interests in relations with Russia seems shortsighted.[15] The alliance can be broadly supported in both countries only if the justification for its existence is shared. If only because of the probable demands of the U.S. public and Congress, the continued viability of Japan's military relationship with the United States must depend in the long run on finding a new basis for the alliance tied, among other things, to a common modus vivendi with Russia. It will therefore be in the common interest if the United States, with due discretion, begins to work informally behind the

---

It should be noted that Dulles did not oppose a two-island deal per se, but only the corollary drawn by Moscow—Japanese recognition of Soviet sovereignty over the two larger islands in dispute. In practice, however, Khrushchev under the best of circumstances would have been unlikely to complete a two-islands settlement without such Japanese recognition.

[15]An embarrassment to the alliance already created by its new Russian problem is the fact that Tokyo may find it awkward politically to explain to the Japanese public the expansion of military cooperation with the United States into any new area that may also involve such cooperation with Russia. One case in point is the proposed Global Protection Against Limited Strikes system (GPALS). The United States has suggested participation in this system to both Yeltsin and Miyazawa, and both may have some security reasons for wishing to participate. But Japanese political leaders may find it difficult to justify publicly such de facto, "parallel" security cooperation with Russia so long as Russia refuses to give back the Northern Territories.

scenes to encourage Japan to renew, and if possible, improve the 1991 Ozawa proposal.

To be sure, there are potential problems attached to such a U.S. effort even aside from the great political obstacles in the Japanese and Russian elites. By the close of 1992, the Russian economic and political crisis—above all, the threat of hyperinflation, the fears of massive unemployment, and the diffusion of authority in Moscow—had grown to such an extent that some would question whether any outside economic assistance could make a major contribution to solving the crisis. Those who hold this highly pessimistic view can only have had their assumptions reinforced by the fall of the reformist Premier Gaidar. In addition, there is a question about the relevant scale of assistance. Some in the West are uncertain whether the $26 billion once offered by Ozawa would now in any case be sufficient to make a meaningful dent in Russia's enormous capital needs, and for that reason have urged Japan to consider larger sums.

There is no doubt that the usefulness of Western and Japanese assistance will turn mostly on the future behavior of the Russians themselves—and to what extent the reform process can survive the events at the December 1992 session of the Congress of People's Deputies. In particular, averting the threat of hyperinflation will be one of several prerequisites for effective Russian use of any future external assistance, including any hypothetical Japanese aid package that might be associated with a territorial settlement. But given a necessary minimum of Russian cooperation, appropriately directed Japanese and Western help could still make an important difference in easing the Russian transition to a market economy. Moreover, the political effects of such inputs from the industrial democracies could be at least as important as the economic effects, by reinforcing the gravely weakened political position of those in the Russian elite who have fought, against increasing odds, for both marketization and friendly ties with the West.[16] In particular, Western and Japanese assistance

---

[16]Some members of the Japanese governing elite accept this point, and therefore intimate that the Japanese government should be less rigid about refusing economic assistance to Russia prior to a territorial settlement. In October 1992, Takujiro Hamada, a former vice foreign minister and an LDP member of parliament, wrote that "foreign aid can help ease the current economic hardships and thereby provide some near-term stability that may support the creation of more permanent democratic institutions." Therefore, Hamada said, "perhaps providing aid to Russia can be treated

is likely to help the Russian political situation to the degree that it is directed toward mitigating the social effects of the unemployment expected to flow from downsizing of large, money-losing military industrial enterprises.[17]

Resurrection of the 1991 Ozawa proposal for a large economic quid pro quo may not elicit an early response from Russia, given the adverse political pressures that now exist there. But it is nevertheless possible that given enough time, a coalition can be created in Moscow willing to bear the massive political burden of territorial concessions if shown a real prospect of a sufficiently massive Russian economic reward. The United States should do what it can to encourage the emergence of such a Russian coalition. But the process of building Russian support for a settlement cannot even begin until Japan becomes willing to speak of a quid pro quo in more than evasive generalities.

In addition—but only in conjunction with the emergence of that economic quid pro quo—the United States should formally reexamine with Japan the question of the confidence-building measures in northeast Asia long advocated by Moscow, which in the past have traditionally been opposed by the United States and Japan as tending to constrain the operations of the alliance. To some extent, this process has already quietly begun, but it would be useful for it to be accelerated, so that the two allies can jointly determine which specific and limited confidence-building measures are acceptable under the radically new strategic circumstances, and which are not.[18] It is in

---

in parallel with efforts to solve the Northern Territories problem." *(International Herald Tribune,* October 6, 1992.)

[17]The fear of such unemployment has been the chief weapon at the disposal of those who have insisted on continued heavy subsidies to such enterprises, thus aggravating the threat of runaway inflation. Note, in this connection, the proposal for a multibillion dollar Western hard-currency "safety net" for such Russian unemployed, advanced by George Soros in late 1992. (*The Wall Street Journal,* November 11, 1992.) The World Bank in late November 1992 approved a $70 million loan for this purpose, but this sum is greatly incommensurate with the scope of the problem. (Reuters, November 24, 1992.)

[18]Although up to now the Japanese elite consensus has not favored using the aid and territorial issues as a vehicle for negotiating a more favorable security environment in northeast Asia, the balance of opinion here could change. Some pro-defense analysts in Japan have advocated using the opportunity to press Moscow for deeper cuts in Russian military deployments in the area, while some members of the Japanese elite

the common interest of Japan and the United States to seek to reduce both the inclination and the ability of the Russian military establishment to obstruct Russian concessions in the region. To this end, it would be helpful for those CBMs found to be consistent with preservation of a viable alliance to be offered to Russia at an early date, provided that this is done against the background of a major Japanese economic offer tacitly linked to a territorial settlement.

IF A SETTLEMENT OCCURS: IMPLICATIONS FOR THE ALLIANCE

We turn finally to the most important long-term contingency facing the alliance, the possibility that despite the vast difficulties that now confront it, a Russo-Japanese territorial settlement will eventually emerge later in this decade. A peace treaty between the two states would presumably soon follow. What would then be the implications for the U.S.-Japanese military alliance?

In the first place, it is obvious that this event would greatly intensify and accelerate the pressures that are already growing to reshape the mission and orientation of the alliance, to make it more open-ended and inevitably less concrete and specific, because it would be less immediately focused on Russia. In other words, to the degree that it had not already done so, the Japanese-American alliance would then have to face directly the kind of fundamental questions about its purpose that the NATO alliance has been forced to confront and debate ever since the collapse of the Soviet Union. Although very important reasons do exist for preserving the U.S. alliance with Japan and for maintaining significant U.S. force deployments in the western Pacific, it may become increasingly difficult to persuade the American public and Congress of this argument if the prolonged Japanese quarrel with Russia imposes an artificial delay in addressing the issue.

---

are evidently now prepared to enter into the multilateral security discussions alluded to by Poltoranin. In October 1992, the former Foreign Ministry official Takujiro Hamada urged "expanding our [Japan-Russia] discussions beyond the bilateral framework and placing the Russian-Japanese relationship in a more regional context. . . . Multilateral talks with a primary focus on security might lead to progress on a peace treaty that includes a territorial settlement." (*International Herald Tribune*, October 6, 1992.) It is not clear, however, how widely this view is shared in Tokyo.

As already suggested, Japan for its part has several strong incentives to want to maintain the alliance.

First, the military alliance with America remains the bulwark of the total Japanese-American relationship, helping to offset the economic tensions that exist between Japan and its most important customer. Not only the Japanese government, but a broad consensus in the Japanese business community seem convinced of this.

Second, the alliance with the United States serves as what might be termed the protective cover for Japan's economic and political relationship with its Asian neighbors. Japan's tie to the United States is generally seen as an insurance policy for East Asia, helping to calm the suspicions and concerns about Japan's strength that exist almost everywhere in the Far East and that would emerge into the open if not for the reassuring perception that a rebirth of Japanese militarism is held in check by Japan's military alliance with America.[19] The Japanese leadership is well aware of this.

And third, the alliance is a guarantee for Japan itself against the unknown: that is, the possibility that some new, presently absent threat will emerge to replace the vanished Soviet threat (e.g., from China, or from a new Sino-Russian alliance, or from a nuclear-armed North Korea).[20] The potential dangers for Japan latent in recent trends in East Asia have been dramatized by the accelerating growth of the arms race in the region, particularly since the demise of the Soviet Union.

The future attitude of the American public and Congress toward the alliance in the face of drastic geopolitical changes and grim budget realities is more problematical. A strong case can be made, however, for continuation of expenditures sufficient to preserve the alliance and maintain some American forward deployments in the region.

---

[19]These widespread East Asian suspicions and fears are perpetuated by the unfortunate refusal of the Japanese governing elite to acknowledge the reality of Japanese behavior during World War II.

[20]The Japan Defense Agency has begun to explore publicly such possible future threats, although the credibility of this search is weakened by the Japanese elite's preference for adhering to an anachronistic hostility toward Russia. See statements attributed to Defense Agency counselor Haruo Ueno in *Los Angeles Times*, September 26, 1992.

Many of the following considerations are analogous to those which suggest why, even after the demise of the Soviet Union, it is also in the U.S. interest to maintain the NATO alliance and to continue some force presence in Europe.

First, the United States itself benefits politically from the fact that most of the East Asian states are quite anxious to see the U.S.-Japanese alliance continue as a guarantee of Japanese political and military restraint. For that very reason, the existence of the alliance fortifies the welcome given by many of those states to the U.S. military presence in the region and increases their self-interest in cooperating with the United States—for example, with support facilities. In addition, many East Asians, like the Japanese, are concerned at the evidence of increasing Chinese assertiveness and the recent accleration of PRC weapons modernization, and welcome the continuation of the U.S. presence as a geopolitical counterweight.[21]   For both reasons, the continuation of an American presence tied to the Japanese alliance enhances U.S. influence in the region.

Second, despite the existence of alternative support facilities elsewhere, the loss of the Philippine bases and the prospect of a reduced presence in Korea has made the Japanese military connection more important than ever for the U.S. geopolitical position in East Asia. The demise of the Japanese alliance would probably mean a general pullback of the United States from the western Pacific.

Third, the United States, like East Asia, should be concerned about regional insurance against the unknown future. Americans, no less than the Japanese, have an interest in preserving the alliance as protection against unpleasant contingencies that may or may not yet be

---

[21]Since the collapse of the Soviet Union, prospects for Chinese force modernization have been significantly enhanced by the multiplication of Russian offers of advanced weapons and military technology for sale at greatly reduced prices. (See *New York Times,* October 18, 1992; *Los Angeles Times,* November 30, 1992.) Premier Gaidar stated in early December that the PRC by then had signed contracts with Russia for more than $1 billion worth of such weaponry and machinery. *(Washington Post,* December 3, 1992.) The Chinese have also entered into agreements to have hundreds of Russian specialists renovate their defense industry, and to have Chinese specialists trained at Russian defense enterprises. (INTERFAX, November 10, 1992; FBIS-SOV, November 13, 1992.)

visible on the horizon.[22]   As in Europe, the Asian alliance of the United States is an investment in defense of American interests that will be affected by unknowable future developments in any case, whether or not U.S. forces remain on the scene.

Finally, the United States, no less than the Asian states, has a national interest in preserving the alliance as a means of ensuring that the Japanese political consensus underlying Japan's restrained and cooperative military posture will endure.   If some day dangerous changes do occur in the Far East, the American relationship with Japan, by reassuring the Japanese public, will reinforce the likelihood of moderation in the Japanese national reaction.   One obvious such contingency would be North Korean achievement of a nuclear capability, which in the absence of the U.S. umbrella might strengthen the hand of the presently small Japanese minority that wishes to do the same.[23]

CONCLUSIONS

The most important conclusion of this report is that delay and lassitude in confronting the difficulties looming in the alliance are likely to be harmful. The world has changed; Japanese and American interests regarding Russia are no longer working in harmony, and indeed are now operating at cross-purposes. The Russo-Japanese dispute, once so convenient to the United States, is now an increasing burden to the Japanese alliance with America. The United States does have an important national interest in the preservation of its alliance with Japan, and for that very reason, although America can

---

[22]Among other things, the United States, like Japan, should be concerned about the long-term dangers that are being created by the growth of the arms race in Asia since the collapse of the Soviet Union. The United States has itself contributed to this arms race, but the biggest single factor has been the creation of a vast Asian arms bazaar from the stocks of the dwindling Soviet Army and from the surplus production of the huge Russian military industrial complex now faced with diminishing demand at home. As noted, China has been the leading customer and beneficiary.

[23]In this connection, some foreign observers have suggested that the Japanese decision to import near-weapons-grade plutonium was intended, among other things, to create a nuclear deterrent without violating Japan's antinuclear principles. In this view, storage of industrial plutonium in Japan was designed to have the side-effect of demonstrating to Japan's neighbors its capability to switch to nuclear weapons production if provoked to do so. (*International Herald Tribune*, November 10, 1992.)

never be a neutral mediator between Russia and Japan, it now has a big stake in a settlement between these two countries.

Notwithstanding all the great difficulties recounted in this report, a settlement is not out of the question, given sufficient will on both sides. Some sizable prerequisites would have to be satisfied regarding changes in both countries. In Russia, *if* Yeltsin survives the present adverse trends and *if* his domestic position should eventually be repaired to some degree by at least modest economic success, his ability to make concessions to Tokyo could then improve—but only if Japan can be induced in the meantime to articulate a reasonably commensurate quid pro quo. A Russian coalition to support a settlement will never be assembled until a Japanese quid pro quo is visible. The first step must therefore necessarily be changes in Japan sufficient to permit the revival—and, indeed, improvement—of the Ozawa offer.

Meanwhile, within the Japanese elite, support for the entrenched official position on the Northern Territories seems to be very gradually declining, especially among younger Japanese. Although this slow secular trend seems unlikely soon to have a decisive effect on the government position, it has already had some modest effects and could have more because of the broader pressures for change now converging on Japan.

In a larger sense, the conservatism and immobility displayed in Japanese strategy toward Yeltsin are manifestations of a more general tendency toward foreign policy inertia. This insularity and passivity was born in the early days of the American postwar protectorate over Japan and became imbedded as Japan prospered during the cold war under the shelter of the American strategic umbrella. Many in the West believe this traditional mind-set has become more and more discordant with reality in recent decades as Japan has become an economic superpower and the bipolar world has disappeared. The "disconnect" between the impact of Japan's economic dynamism upon the world and the torpidity of its external political behavior has evoked increasing complaints from Japan's interlocutors, including the United States. Examples in recent years have included the friction that grew out of Japan's unenthusiastic attitude toward the 1991 Gulf war, as well as the dismayed reaction of some Americans to the "low posture" Japan adopted in the General

Agreement on Tariffs and Trade (GATT) negotiations, in whose outcome Japan has as large a stake as anyone.

It is true, of course, that there are objective constraints on changes in this pattern of behavior, some of them external to Japan. Japan's neighbors share with much of Japan's population great concern over the possibility that more active Japanese political and security involvement overseas could presage a rebirth of Japanese militarism. These concerns were reflected in the long struggle over Japanese participation in UN peacekeeping operations in Cambodia. Moreover, Japanese policymakers rightly note that the West is reluctant to cede to Tokyo the formal role in international security decision-making—notably, a permanent seat on the UN Security Council—that seems to the Japanese both appropriate to Japan's international stature and an inevitable consequence of Japan's assumption of the greater international responsibilities for which some in the West are pressing.

The other powers' evasion of this question up to now has, to be sure, stemmed from more than mere reluctance to give the Japanese their due. Acquiescence in Japan's claim to a permanent seat on the Security Council would probably require agreement to Germany's equally valid claim, and might also precipitate a struggle over the claims of a long list of other aspirants. It might also open the way for demands for revision of the structure and membership of the Security Council for reasons of geographical balance. It is therefore not surprising that the present permanent members have up to now preferred to defer the issue.

Nevertheless, it seems likely that watershed changes of this kind will indeed come to pass in this decade, and that they will eventually have a substantial effect on Japanese behavior in the world arena as well as on the configuration of forces within the Japanese elite. It is difficult to believe that a breakthrough into a new position of formal international responsibility will not in the end strengthen the hand of those younger forces in Japanese society—and in the LDP—that have begun to struggle for a fundamental transformation of the Japanese policy formulation process. One of the key decisions demanded by the new situation will be to put an end to the tradition of complaisant drift in policy toward Russia. The United States should do what it can to facilitate and accelerate that change.